CPG

cherbo publishing group, inc.

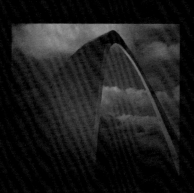

MISSOURI

Gateway to Enterprise

KRISTINA SAUERWEIN

DEDICATION

To Tom Geiser, my husband, my best friend, my all.

ACKNOWLEDGMENTS

I give special thanks to Cherbo Publishing Group and the Missouri Department of Economic Development for making this book possible. In particular, I extend my gratitude to my editor, Erica Rheinschild, for her keen eye, kind manner, and careful editing of the manuscript. I appreciate the support of Margaret Martin, managing editor, who granted me the opportunity to write this book. I am also indebted to Tina Rubin, senior editor and my writing friend, for introducing me to Cherbo Publishing Group and encouraging me to take on this project.

Additionally, I'd like to recognize workers at the Missouri businesses and organizations in this book. I am grateful for the time they took out of their busy schedules to share their expertise during interviews, as well as for providing me with resources such as annual reports, on-line information, fact sheets, economic forecasts, and executive summaries. I am honored to chronicle the achievements of the people of Missouri.

Finally, I am thankful to my family: my parents for reveling in my writing and my in-laws for their enthusiasm and experiences as lifelong Missouri residents, which helped to shape the book.

 cherbo publishing group, inc.

PRESIDENT	JACK C. CHERBO	ART DIRECTOR	PERI A. HOLGUIN
EXECUTIVE VICE PRESIDENT	ELAINE HOFFMAN	DESIGNER	THEODORE E. YEAGER
EDITORIAL DIRECTOR	CHRISTINA M. BEAUSANG	PROFILES DESIGNER	JOEL VENDETTE
MANAGING FEATURE EDITOR	MARGARET L. MARTIN	SENIOR PHOTO EDITOR	AMY JUDA
FEATURE EDITOR	ERICA RHEINSCHILD	PHOTO EDITOR	WALTER MLADINA
SENIOR PROFILES EDITOR	J. KELLEY YOUNGER	DIGITAL COLOR SPECIALIST	ART VASQUEZ
PROFILES EDITORS	BROOS CAMPBELL	SALES ADMINISTRATOR	JOAN K. BAKER
	LIZA YETENEKIAN SMITH	PRODUCTION SERVICES COORDINATOR	PATRICIA DE LEONARD
ASSOCIATE EDITOR	SYLVIA EMRICH-TOMA	PRODUCTION SERVICES ASSISTANT	LESLIÉ E. SHAW
PROFILE WRITERS	MARY C. MARSHALL	ADMINISTRATIVE ASSISTANT	BILL WAY
	BETH MATTSON-TIEG	SOUTHWEST REGIONAL MANAGER	JOHN HECKER
	PAUL SONNENBURG	PUBLICATIONS DIRECTOR	BOB FREEMAN
	PENNY SUESS	PUBLICATIONS COORDINATORS	KATHY M. KENNEDY
	JASON WROBLEWSKI		SUSAN SMITH
	LIZA YETENEKIAN-SMITH		
	STAN ZIEMBA		

Cherbo Publishing Group, Inc., Encino, Calif. 91316
© 2004 by Cherbo Publishing Group, Inc.
All rights reserved. Published 2004
Printed by Friesens
Altona, Manitoba, Canada
Neche, North Dakota, USA

Library of Congress cataloging-in-publication data
Sauerwein, Kristina
A pictorial guide highlighting 19th-through-21st-century
Missouri economic and social history.
Library of Congress control number: 2004100706
ISBN 1-882933-57-5

Visit the CPG Web site at www.cherbopub.com.

CONTENTS

MISSOURI ORIGINALS 4
Historic Highlights

PART ONE PURSUING THE AMERICAN DREAM: LIVING AND WORKING IN MISSOURI 12
CHAPTER 1 EXPLORING THE POSSIBILITIES 14
Quality of Life

PART TWO CHANGING THE WORLD: MISSOURI'S ENTREPRENEURS AND INNOVATORS 30
CHAPTER 2 FERTILE BEGINNINGS, A BOUNTIFUL FUTURE 32
Agriculture, Food Processing, Mining, and Forestry

CHAPTER 3 A LEGACY OF LEARNING 42
Education

CHAPTER 4 BUILDING ASSETS 52
Finance, Insurance, Real Estate, and Construction

CHAPTER 5 MODERN MEDICINE 62
Health Care and Biotechnology

CHAPTER 6 ON THE CUTTING EDGE 72
Information Technology, Communications, and the Media

CHAPTER 7 MADE IN MISSOURI 82
Manufacturing

CHAPTER 8 GETTING DOWN TO BUSINESS 92
Professional and Business-to-Business Services

CHAPTER 9 DESTINATION MISSOURI 100
Tourism, Hospitality, and Retail

CHAPTER 10 MOVING FORWARD 110
Transportation, Utilities, and Energy

PART THREE PORTRAITS OF SUCCESS: PROFILES OF CORPORATIONS AND ORGANIZATIONS 120

CORPORATIONS AND ORGANIZATIONS PROFILED

The following corporations and organizations have made a valuable commitment to the quality of this publication. The Missouri Department of Economic Development gratefully acknowledges their participation in *Missouri: Gateway to Enterprise.*

Andy's Seasoning, Inc. 130
Anheuser-Busch Companies, Inc. 128–29
Bayer CropScience 27, 174–75
BioKyowa Inc. 173
Blue Cross and Blue Shield of Missouri 150
Blue Springs School District 139
Central Missouri State University 18, 134–35
Charter Communications, Inc. 26, 166–67
City of Kansas City, Missouri 124–25
Express Scripts 162–63
General Motors Corp. 176–77
George K. Baum & Company 146
Hellmuth, Obata + Kassabaum, Inc. 180
Kansas City Airport Marriott 192
Kansas City Aviation Department 198
Lambert–St. Louis International Airport 21, 196–97
Lindenwood University 140
Maverick Tube Corporation 170–72
Missouri Credit Union Association 20, 144–45
Missouri Hospital Association 154–55
Missouri Western State College 138
St. Louis Rams 188
Saint Luke's Health System 19, 156–57
Southeast Missouri Hospital 22, 158–59
Southwest Missouri State University 23, 136–37
UniGroup, Inc. 199
Worlds of Fun 184

GREETINGS:

Missourians have always exemplified a progressive, determined spirit and strong midwestern work ethic that has become our state's trademark. As we continue to make the transition into the new millennium, there is no better time to reflect on how our state has grown, where we have been, where we are now, and where we are going.

From our roots in agriculture and manufacturing to our current life sciences and auto industries, the story of Missouri's enterprise is a true reflection of the great strides we have made as a state. In the 1800s, Missouri was the starting point for pioneers who were seeking an exciting, new life on the western frontier, a life that promised new adventures and endless opportunities. Of course, there have been many technological advances and changes since then, but the same pioneer spirit exists today. I am proud of the spirit, leadership, and commitment that Missouri's businesses, communities, and residents demonstrate by always striving to improve, explore new opportunities, and enrich the quality of life for all of us.

With its central location, diverse economy, low cost of living, and highly motivated and well-trained workforce, Missouri is poised to be a leader in the 21st century. We are blessed with an abundance of natural resources that have enabled us to maximize our potential and increase our promise for growth.

We can be proud of what we have built and what we have achieved. Our history is rich with landmark accomplishments and events, and our future is rich with the potential of exciting possibilities.

Missouri boasts a strong spirit of enterprise and community, as proven by the stories of individuals and businesses contained in these pages. I invite you to read Missouri's story and let us show you all that the Show-Me State has to offer.

Sincerely,

Bob Holden
Governor

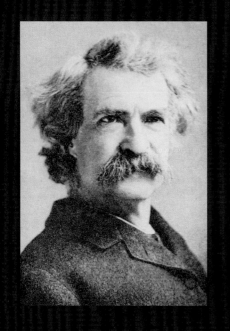

MISSOURI ORIGINALS

From AstroTurf, air-conditioning, and ATM/credit cards to shopping centers, saccharin, and sliced bread, Missouri's innovations and triumphs illustrate the state's diversity and creativity. Its pioneering spirit and ingenious entrepreneurs have helped the Show-Me State to flourish.

1835 Samuel Langhorne Clemens, also known as Mark Twain, is born in Florida, Missouri. He becomes a major American author, writing classics such as *The Adventures of Tom Sawyer* in 1876 and *Adventures of Huckleberry Finn* in 1884.

1857 Harris Teachers College in St. Louis becomes the first education institution for public teachers west of the Mississippi River.

1821 Missouri is admitted as the 24th state on August 10th.

1821

1846

1857

1824 St. Regis Seminary, the nation's first Roman Catholic institution for the higher education of Native Americans, opens in Florissant.

1846 Dred Scott, a slave, sues for his freedom at the St. Louis courthouse. Scott wins in circuit court, however, the U.S. Supreme Court rules against him in 1857. The decision sets the stage for the Civil War.

1859 The Missouri School for the Blind in St. Louis introduces Braille to the Western Hemisphere.

1860 The Pony Express starts its first route from St. Joseph. From there, a relay of horse riders carries mail saddlebags across a 2,000-mile trail.

1873 The St. Louis Board of Education creates the country's first public kindergarten class.

1876 Anheuser-Busch in St. Louis unveils Budweiser, which becomes the best-selling beer in the United States.

1891 Almon Brown Strowger patents the first automated telephone exchange in Kansas City. Strowger's product enables callers to make a direct connection without an operator.

1899 Ragtime musician Scott Joplin plays at the Maple Leaf Club in Sedalia, inspiring store owner John Stark to buy Joplin's *Maple Leaf Rag* for $50 plus royalties. The composition is one of the first pieces of American sheet music to sell more than a million copies.

1873   *1891*

1869   *1889*   *1901*

1869 Washington University in St. Louis is one of the first universities in the United States to admit a woman to its law school. That student, Phoebe Wilson Couzins, graduates from the school and becomes the country's first female federal marshal, in 1887.

1874 The world's first steel truss bridge, built across the Mississippi River in St. Louis, is completed.

1889 Thomas Hart Benton, a pioneer in "regionalist" painting, is born in Neosho. In 1936, he paints the *Missouri State Capitol* series in the capitol building in Jefferson City.

1894 Twenty-seven-year-old Laura Ingalls Wilder settles in Mansfield with her family. At age 65, she begins writing the beloved *Little House on the Prairie* series of children's novels, which is adapted to television in the 1970s to great success.

1901 Dr. Charles Stark Draper, known as the "father of inertial navigation," is born in Windsor. The technology he invents is used in aircraft, submarines, and spacecraft.

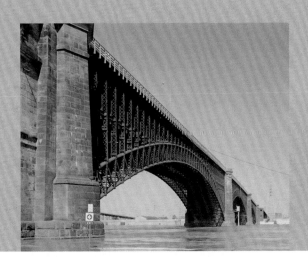

MISSOURI ORIGINALS

1902 Monsanto in St. Louis manufactures the first saccharin product. It is shipped to Coca-Cola, a growing soft drink company in Georgia.

1906 Walt Disney's family moves to Marceline when he is a young boy. Disney becomes a pioneer in animation film production and creates theme parks worldwide that feature a Main Street USA modeled after his small-town childhood home.

1908 Walter Williams founds the world's first school of journalism at the University of Missouri–Columbia.

1918 St. Louis native Sara Teasdale wins the first Pulitzer Prize for Poetry for *Love Songs*.

1902

1908

1907

1921

1904 The Louisiana Purchase Exposition World's Fair in St. Louis opens with the manufacturing and selling of hot dogs and ice-cream cones for the first time. Iced tea, air-conditioning, and the automatic turnstile are also introduced at the fair.

St. Louis hosts the first Olympic Games in the United States.

The St. Louis Police Department is the first in the country to adopt the fingerprinting system.

1907 Charles Eames, noted architect and designer, is born in St. Louis. In 1946, he creates a chair with his wife, Ray Kaiser, that becomes the prototype for mass-produced seating during the mid-century.

1912 Captain Albert Berry makes the first parachute jump from an airplane, at Jefferson Barracks in St. Louis.

1921 Missouri's first radio station, WEW at Saint Louis University, broadcasts.

1922 Country Club Plaza, the nation's first shopping center designed for automobile drivers, opens in Kansas City.

St. Louis–born Thomas Stearns (T. S.) Eliot publishes *The Waste Land,* considered by many to be the most influential body of poetry during the 20th century. Eliot wins the Nobel Prize for Literature in 1948.

1926 The St. Louis Cardinals win their first World Series, defeating the New York Yankees. The Cardinals win the series again in 1931, 1934, 1942, 1944, 1946, 1964, 1967, and 1982.

Hannibal honors former resident Mark Twain with bronze statues of Tom Sawyer and Huckleberry Finn, the first-ever sculptures of literary characters.

1928 A baker in Chillicothe is the first to offer sliced bread for sale.

1930 The Lewis Howe Co. in St. Louis introduces Tums, an antacid calcium supplement used to treat heartburn.

An icon of Americana—the curb service tray—is born at the Parkmoor, a drive-in restaurant in St. Louis.

1944 The nation elects U.S. Senator Harry S. Truman, a native of Independence, to the vice presidency.

1922   *1928*   *1944*

1927   *1943*

1924 The Kansas City Monarchs become champions at the first Negro World Series.

1927 St. Louis businessmen finance Charles Lindbergh's *Spirit of St. Louis* flight from New York to France, the first solo, nonstop flight across the Atlantic Ocean.

1929 Charles Leiper Grigg concocts Bib-Label Lithiated Lemon-Lime Soda in St. Louis. The soda evolves into 7UP, one of the nation's most popular soft drinks.

1943 The George Washington Carver National Monument in Diamond honors the Missourian who was once a slave and became one of the country's most esteemed and prolific scientists. It is the nation's first such tribute to an African-American.

1945 Truman becomes the 33rd U.S. president after Franklin D. Roosevelt dies in office. During his first term, Truman authorizes the atomic bombing of Hiroshima and Nagasaki, Japan, and helps to devise the Marshall Plan.

1946 Winston Churchill gives his legendary Iron Curtain speech at Westminster College in Fulton.

McDonnell Aircraft in St. Louis introduces the FH-1 Phantom, the first U.S. jet to operate from an aircraft carrier.

The country's first commercial mobile telephone service is inaugurated in St. Louis.

1948 The nation elects Truman as president. During his second term, he helps to forge the North Atlantic Treaty Organization (NATO). In 1950, Truman orders American troops into South Korea; the Korean War lasts three years.

Stan Musial, an outfielder for the St. Louis Cardinals, wins the Most Valuable Player Award for the third time. He is the first baseball player to achieve this.

1950s The Midwest Research Institute in Kansas City creates instant coffee, along with a brewing device that is a precursor to modern automatic drip coffeemakers, for the J. A. Folger Company. Scientists also develop the M&M's candy coating that "melts in your mouth, not in your hand."

1956 The nation's first interstate highway project starts in Missouri.

1946 *1950*

1949 *1957*

1947 Doctors Carl Ferdinand Cori and Gerty Theresa Cori of Washington University's School of Medicine win a Nobel Prize for their discovery of how sugar is converted into glycogen in humans.

1949 The nation's first all-electric railroad dining car, the Café St. Louis, commences service between St. Louis and Chicago.

1953 Hallmark in Kansas City produces Christmas cards for President and Mrs. Dwight D. Eisenhower, who send the first U.S. presidential Christmas cards.

1957 Phillip Sollomi, owner of The Wish-Bone restaurant in Kansas City, sells his now-famous salad dressing to the Thomas J. Lipton Company.

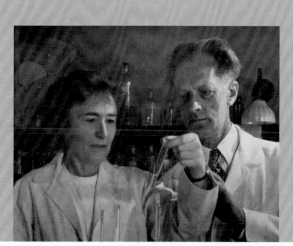

1960 Theodore McNeal becomes Missouri's first African-American state senator. He advocates for civil rights, fair employment practices, and the creation of the University of Missouri–St. Louis.

1963 AMC Entertainment in Kansas City opens the world's first multi-screen theater in a Kansas City mall.

1965 Workers complete the Gateway Arch in St. Louis, the nation's tallest monument at 630 feet high.

1969 Silver Dollar City's re-creation of an 1800s mining town in Branson attracts Hollywood producers to film parts of *The Beverly Hillbillies* television series there.

1971 Ralston Purina Company in St. Louis manufactures Tender Vittles, the first moist cat food.

A Stetson hat manufacturing plant opens in St. Joseph, producing up to 2,000 hats daily. The facility is one of the nation's largest hat-makers, attracting thousands of tourists each year.

Rival Manufacturing Company in Kansas City introduces the world's first Crock-Pot.

1960 **1964** **1965** **1970** **1971**

1961 Alan Shepard is the first American to barrel into space, inside the Mercury MR-3 spacecraft, built by the McDonnell Company. In 1962, the company's Mercury MA-6 carries John Glenn, the first American to orbit the earth. In 1965, McDonnell's Gemini 4 carries Ed White, the first American to walk in space.

1964 The country's first automated library circulation system is installed at the University of Missouri–Columbia.

1966 Monsanto's AstroTurf, the first synthetic grass, is installed at the AstroDome in Houston. AstroTurf becomes a staple in stadiums and sports arenas worldwide.

1970 James Fergason, a Wakenda native, invents the first operating liquid crystal display (LCD). His discovery leads to the use of LCDs in digital clocks, calculators, computer monitors, and more.

1972 The Midwest's first successful heart transplant occurs at Saint Louis University's Health Sciences Center, making it one of three institutions in the United States pioneering this procedure.

1975 Washington University researchers detail how taking aspirin can help to prevent heart attacks.

1977 The Midwest Research Institute is contracted to operate the U.S. Department of Energy's Solar Energy Research Institute, making it the nation's leading center for renewable energy research.

1983 President Ronald Reagan declares September 22nd "American Business Women's Day" in honor of the American Business Women's Association in Kansas City and the country's working women.

1985 The Kansas City Royals defeat the St. Louis Cardinals in the World Series. The sporting event is nicknamed the "I-70 Series" for the interstate highway that connects the two cities.

1975　　　　　　　　　　　　1983

　　　　1982　　　　　　　　　　　　1986

1976 Boxers Michael and Leon Spinks from St. Louis compete at the Summer Olympics in Montreal and are the first brothers to win gold medals in the same sport at the same Olympics.

1982 Monsanto scientists make history by being the first to genetically modify a plant cell.

1984 Commerce Bank in Kansas City offers the first card that functions as a credit and ATM card.

1986 St. Louis–born Chuck Berry is the first person inducted into the Rock 'n' Roll Hall of Fame.

1989 Monsanto produces Cytotec, the world's first anti-ulcer medication.

1993 Monsanto introduces Posilac bovine somatotropin, the world's largest selling dairy animal health product.

1997 Saint Louis University's School of Nursing becomes the first in the country to offer a master's degree program for nurse practitioners entirely on the World Wide Web.

Mergers create Ameren Corporation in St. Louis, and its main operating companies, AmerenUE and AmerenCIPS. It is Missouri's largest electric utility.

2000 The St. Louis Rams win the Super Bowl, defeating the Tennessee Titans.

2004 Ophthalmologists at Washington University School of Medicine demonstrate a key risk factor in the development of cataracts. For the first time, they link the gel found between the back of the eye lens and the retina to the occurrence of nuclear cataracts, the most common type of age-related cataracts.

1989   *1997*   *2004*

1995   *2002*

1990 Missouri's first Miss America, Debbye Turner, dons her crown.

1995 Interstate Bakeries Corporation in Kansas City ranks as the nation's top wholesale baker, selling familiar brands such as Wonder, Hostess, and Home Pride.

1998 Hoechst Marion Roussel in Kansas City introduces Allegra-D, a nondrowsy antihistamine for seasonal allergy relief.

On September 8th, St. Louis Cardinals' first baseman Mark McGwire hits his 62nd home run of the season, breaking Roger Maris's record. Three weeks later, McGwire bests his record with his 70th home run.

2002 The Botanical Society of America moves its headquarters from Ohio to St. Louis, an acknowledgment of the region's importance in plant and life sciences.

PART ONE

PURSUING THE AMERICAN DREAM

Living and Working in Missouri

EXPLORING THE POSSIBILITIES
Quality of Life

In 1804, Meriwether Lewis and William Clark led an expedition starting along the Missouri River, near St. Louis, and ending in the Northwest at the Pacific Ocean. The untapped terrain, known as the Louisiana Purchase, provided locations for forts, trading posts, and ultimately, a higher quality of life for residents in Missouri as well as the United States.

Two centuries later, Missouri continues to be a place of exploration and innovation. Its pioneering spirit, centrality, and natural resources have produced the nation's fifth most diversified economy, with strong performance in sectors such as wholesale trade, construction, manufacturing, transportation, communications, and public utilities. From stalwart industries to

advancing fields, the state remains an important global player, poised for progress and possibilities.

STATE OF GROWTH

Approximately 5.7 million people call Missouri home. The state's population is the 17th largest in the United States, with Caucasians and African-Americans accounting for the top two ethnic majorities. A low cost of

Above: Built in the 1960s to commemorate the Louisiana Purchase, the Gateway Arch in St. Louis is a Missouri icon. Each year, more than one million people go to the top of the arch to enjoy a panoramic view of the city. **Left:** Lewis and Clark's journey of discovery, which began near St. Louis, took the explorers more than 8,000 miles through the American West.

living, a range of job opportunities, and a solid economy are attracting thousands of newcomers each year, including those from countries such as Mexico, Vietnam, and Bosnia. Latinos, who are establishing roots in places like Kansas City, St. Louis, Springfield, Carthage, and Fort Leonard Wood, comprise Missouri's most rapidly growing population. Like the state's early settlers, new residents are contributing to Missouri's financial health and cultural diversity.

The state is also attracting companies, nonprofits, and educational institutions that explore new realms. In 2003, the state boasted 12 Fortune 500 companies, employing approximately 26,000 people and paying wages totaling more than $1.1 billion. Emerson, headquartered in St. Louis, was the state's top-ranking Fortune 500 company that year. Three other St. Louis–based companies—Anheuser-Busch, May Department Stores Company, and Charter Communications—along with Carthage-based Leggett & Platt, were not far behind on the list. Among *Fortune* magazine's "100 Fastest Growing Companies" were First Banks America in Clayton, Engineered Support Systems in St. Louis, and Express Scripts in Maryland Heights.

In October 2003, 1,272 companies started in Missouri, representing a significant jump from the same month in the previous year. Mirroring the state's diversified economy, new business spread throughout the state and varied from service industries, construction, and wholesale trade to insurance, finance, and real estate. Missouri also witnessed an increase in new manufacturing firms, despite a severe nationwide slump in the sector.

Besides being a sound place for businesses to establish headquarters, Missouri has assets that have convinced out-of-state companies to establish offices, subsidiaries, warehousing sites, and manufacturing plants in the state. Chicago-based Boeing Company, for instance, runs several multimillion-dollar divisions in St. Louis, making it one of the area's top employers.

NATURE'S BOUNTY

The state's natural resources also elevate its economic relevance. The

Above: Kansas City's Country Club Plaza inspired developers nationwide when it was built in 1922. Today, it continues to delight people with shops, restaurants, and seasonal events. Opposite page: Once the largest rail station in the world, Union Station in St. Louis is now a busy shopping, dining, and entertainment destination. The 1894 building was renovated in 1985.

Bobby R. Patton, Ph.D.
President,
Central Missouri
State University

Central Missouri State University is not only a vital educational resource for residents of the west central part of the state, as it prepares more than 2,000 graduates annually to enter the workforce, but also a strong contributor to the area economically and culturally. The university is the second largest employer in Johnson County, Missouri, with approximately 1,125 full-time faculty and staff members, in addition to numerous student workers.

Offering guest speakers, art events, musical concerts by student and professional performers, and theatrical events, including the summer Central Missouri Repertory, the university is truly a cultural and artistic hub for the area.

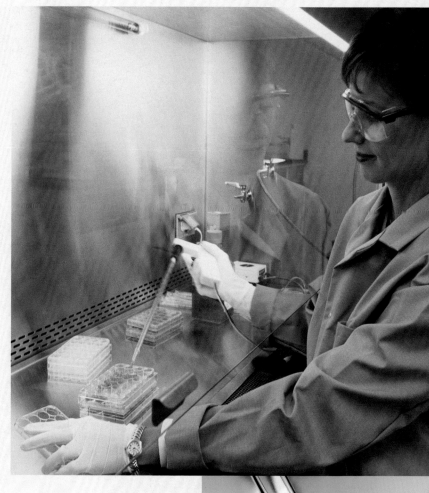

land in southeastern Missouri alone supplies an estimated 70 percent of the nation's primary lead. Also in abundance is the Eastern black walnut tree, whose nutmeats taste good and whose shells are processed for paints, cosmetics, explosives, oil well drilling, and metal cleaning.

Missouri's diverse topography, irrigation sources, and climates propel its agricultural prominence. It is the nation's second leading state in beef operations, number of farms, and hay production, excluding alfalfa. In 2002, the state's 107,000 farms sold an estimated $4.4 billion in crops, aquaculture, and poultry and livestock, the latter of which comprised more than half of the state's agricultural output.

Missouri has also distinguished itself as a global hot spot in plant and life sciences. The new millennium

Bob Holden earmarked 25 percent of the proceeds from the state's future tobacco settlement to establish a Life Sciences Research Trust Fund and a Center for Excellence in Life Sciences Research, with locations in St. Louis, Springfield, and Kansas City.

The Life Sciences Research Trust Fund is one example of how

G. Richard Hastings
President and CEO,
Saint Luke's Health System

Missouri has many claims to fame, from its quality of life to its beautiful scenery. But perhaps one of the best reasons to live in Missouri is the quality of our health care.

At Saint Luke's Health System, we are proud to play a vital role in protecting and preserving the health of the people of our region. We have received national recognition for being on the leading edge of health care, helping to ensure that the people of the communities we serve have access to the very best quality of care available anywhere.

As our state grows and prospers, we look forward to helping to make certain that Missouri has a healthy future.

marked a surge of firms specializing in this industry, which includes commercial biological research, botanical and zoological gardens, testing laboratories, and arboreta. Monsanto in St. Louis is a powerhouse in the field. In 2002, the Botanical Society of America relocated its headquarters from Columbus, Ohio, to St. Louis, signifying the region's growing reputation as the Silicon Valley of plant sciences. That reputation was further enhanced in 2003, when Missouri Governor

Missouri's government and business leaders are ensuring that conditions remain ripe for entrepreneurs. The state has demonstrated its commitment to development by establishing resource networks, financial programs, and higher education programs, including Saint Louis University's award-winning Web site on entrepreneurship.

LIVING IN THE SHOW-ME STATE
Bustling economic activity in Missouri translates into a comfortable

saintlukeshealthsystem.org

This page, left: Missouri's aquaculture industry is growing, with more than 35 species of fish and aquatic plants produced in the state. Opposite page, top right and bottom: Exciting life and plant sciences research is being conducted at Missouri's leading hospitals, universities, and companies.

Roshara Holub
*President and CEO,
Missouri Credit
Union Association*

The Missouri Credit Union Association is fortunate to represent credit unions from all areas of the state. From the urban to the rural areas, Missouri offers a wide variety of opportunities, scenery, traditions, and culture.

Just like the regions of Missouri, credit unions have individual traits that make them unique. But no matter where one goes in the state, the commitment of credit unions to their members and to helping their communities is a constant.

This commitment is very apparent in our work with the Children's Miracle Network (CMN). This organization serves more than 14 million children in 170 CMN-affiliated children's hospitals.

Missouri credit unions, through the CMN Credit Unions for Kids program, raise hundreds of thousands of dollars each year to benefit sick children in our local hospitals.

Helping Missouri's children through CMN Credit Unions for Kids is a perfect fit with the credit union philosophy of "people helping people."

MISSOURI CREDIT UNION ASSOCIATION

lifestyle for many residents. In 2002, Missouri ranked 18th in the nation for total personal income. It also achieved the country's 18th lowest cost of living, which factors in necessities such as housing, groceries, utilities, transportation, and health care.

Missouri offers some of the nation's best medical care. BJC HealthCare in St. Louis, one of the country's largest nonprofits and a top employer in the state, consistently receives high rankings in *U.S. News & World Report's* annual guide to "America's Best Hospitals." Groundbreaking medical research being conducted throughout the state also keeps Missouri on the leading edge. In St. Louis, the Central Institute for the Deaf, a renowned research institution for

cochlear implants, is working on devices to mitigate hearing loss. Two esteemed research facilities in Kansas City—Stowers Institute for Medical Research and the Midwest Research Institute—are charting new paths in cancer and disease research, genetics, the environment, drug development, automation technology, and more.

Education in Missouri also stands out. In 2003, 176 school districts received recognition from the Missouri State Board of Education for improving performance on standardized tests, dropout and attendance rates, and other measures of success. The award increased by 15 districts from the prior year. The U.S. Department of Education, the U.S. Secretary of Education, and magazines such as

This page, right: In the 2002–2003 academic year, the University of Missouri–Columbia had students from every county in Missouri, all 50 states, and more than 100 countries. Opposite page, left: Missouri high school students consistently test higher than their national counterparts on the ACT and SAT exams.

Leonard L. Griggs Jr.
*Director,
Lambert–St. Louis
International Airport*

Business Week, Money Magazine, and *Redbook* frequently honor Missouri's elementary and secondary schools. Indeed, Missouri students traditionally hover above or at the national average when tested against peers in academic subjects such as reading and writing.

More than two-thirds of the state's 18- to 24-year-olds have received, or are working to obtain, high school and college degrees. Students pursuing higher education need not look any further than Missouri's boundaries. More than 360,000 students study at the state's 120 proprietary schools, 25 independent colleges and universities, 13 public four-year colleges and universities, 19 public two-year schools, and one public two-year technical college.

A Tapestry of Culture

From the Kansas City Ballet to the Albrecht-Kemper Museum of Art to the Saint Louis Symphony Orchestra, dance, art, and music are everywhere

For St. Louis, it has always been about "location, location, location." Originally, the confluence of two major rivers attracted French fur trappers, who were looking to establish a trading post in the area. Then, being in the heart of a developing continent contributed to St. Louis's emergence as a hub for river, rail, and highway transportation.

It was aviation, however— initially fascinating to the people and soon recognized for its commercial applications— that established St. Louis as a gateway city for commerce and enterprise. The city of St. Louis's acquisition of Lambert Field in the late 1920s reflected the importance of aviation to the growth of the local economy. The current runway expansion project demonstrates our continuing commitment to Lambert, which is conveniently located at the center of the region's population base.

James W. Wente, CHE, CPA

President and CEO,
Southeast Missouri Hospital

Southeast Missouri Hospital is
located in Cape Girardeau, a
community of 40,000 situated
halfway between St. Louis,
Missouri, and Memphis,
Tennessee. Just a few blocks
from the hospital is Southeast
Missouri State University, with
an enrollment of approximately
9,000 students.

Founded more than 75
years ago, Southeast Missouri
Hospital stands as a prime
example of civic dedication to
health care and quality of life.

At Southeast Missouri
Hospital, we believe it is our
responsibility to be an active
participant in projects that
focus on improving the overall
health and quality of life where
we live and work.

Our commitment to
excellence at Southeast
Missouri Hospital is also a
commitment to the good health
of this community and the
region we serve.

© SMSU Photographic Services

John H. Keiser
President,
Southwest Missouri
State University

There has never been a great
state without great universities.
For 100 years, Southwest
Missouri State University has
been opening the doors of
opportunity for students across
the state.

Today, SMSU is distinguished
by its statewide mission in
public affairs, a campuswide
commitment to foster competence
and responsibility in the common
vocation of citizenship. In the
tradition of John Adams, Thomas
Jefferson, and Benjamin Franklin,
the faculty, staff, and students
of SMSU look for ways to understand and to implement public
affairs, because this is essential
to the future of our state
and nation.

Toward this end, SMSU
graduates "citizen scholars"—
citizen teachers, citizen accountants, citizen nurses, and so on—
to meet the needs of Missouri in
the 21st century.

in Missouri. For more than 45 years, the respected Kansas City Ballet has staged world premieres and classics. Dancers tour the state's rural areas, perform workshops, and teach students about the genre. Kansas City also claims one of the nation's top art institutions, the Nelson-Atkins Museum of Art. It houses collections of European, American, African, and Asian art dating back more than 5,000 years. The museum hopes to enhance its status with a 160,000-square-foot expansion, led by Steven

Holl, an internationally acclaimed architect. The expansion is slated for completion in 2006. North of Kansas City, the Albrecht-Kemper Museum of Art in St. Joseph showcases American art from the 18th, 19th, and 20th centuries. Its collections include works by artists such as William Merritt Chase, Mary Cassatt, and Thomas Hart Benton.

The Saint Louis Symphony Orchestra invigorates people with its esteemed ensemble, producing clas-sical as well as eclectic music. Its

This page, left: Some of the world's biggest stars have performed at the Fox Theatre in St. Louis, including Bob Hope, the Glenn Miller Orchestra, Mae West, and the Grateful Dead. Opened in 1929, the theater continues to host headline talent. Opposite page, right: Each summer, the Shakespeare Festival of St. Louis brings classic theater to thousands of people in Forest Park for free.

Above: The Nelson-Atkins Museum of Art in Kansas City boasts the world's largest collection of works by Missouri artists Thomas Hart Benton and George Caleb Bingham. Shown is Benton's *Palisades,* circa 1919–1924. Opposite page: Some of Benton's most famous murals are inside the Missouri State Capitol in Jefferson City. The capitol also houses the Missouri State Museum.

home is the historic Powell Symphony Hall, hailed as one of the nation's finest music houses. The hall is the centerpiece of a multimillion-dollar performing arts district near downtown St. Louis that includes upscale restaurants, jazz clubs, the Fox Theatre, and Sheldon Memorial Concert Hall.

Along the St. Louis riverfront lies the Jefferson National Expansion Memorial, composed of the Gateway Arch, Old Courthouse, and Museum of Westward Expansion. Forest Park in St. Louis encompasses an array of cultural activities, including the Saint Louis Art Museum, Missouri History Museum, and the Municipal Opera, which hosts summer theater productions in its 12,000-seat outdoor amphitheater.

Smaller, but not less important, cultural destinations sprinkle the state's landscape. The Pony Express Museum in St. Joseph focuses on the Old West's most famous cross-country mail service. Jefferson City offers visitors lessons about the state capital through guided tours of the Missouri State Capitol and the Cole County Historical Museum. Statewide, other exhibits are

Carl E. Vogel

*President and CEO,
Charter Communications, Inc.*

Charter Communications, Inc.,
is dedicated to the more than
4,500 communities we serve in
37 states. In Missouri, we have
500,000 customers in more than
100 cities, including St. Louis, our
headquarters location.

Charter invests financial and
human resources to strengthen
our communities. Throughout
our ranks, we have developed
programs and initiatives—
with countless volunteers and
many charitable contributions
and sponsorships—that provide
groups and organizations with
valuable television time via our
hybrid fiber coaxial networks.
Charter works with communities
to enhance people's quality of
life. Emphasizing education
outreach, we provide free
commercial-free video programming and high-speed Internet
access in the classroom at
public and private schools across
the country.

We are proud to be a builder
and catalyst for innovation.

dedicated to Missouri's famous sons
and daughters, including the Mark
Twain Boyhood Home and
Museum in Hannibal, Walt Disney's
Home Town Museum in Marceline,
the Harry S. Truman Library in
Independence, the Daniel Boone
Home in Defiance, and the Jesse
James Bank Museum in Liberty.

Athletics are another favorite
pastime. It is no coincidence that *The
Sporting News* calls Missouri home.
Headquartered in St. Louis, the
media company publishes a weekly

magazine and commemorative sports
books, operates a popular Web site,
and airs a premier sports-talk radio
network. Fan enthusiasm abounds for
the state's college and professional
leagues, whether spectators don
maroon to support the Southwest
Missouri State Bears basketball team
in Springfield or blue and gold for
the St. Louis Rams, champions of the
2000 Super Bowl. Missourians are
also proud of the St. Louis Blues
hockey team, which has played in
every Stanley Cup playoff for the past

Dr. Dietmar B. Westphal
Senior Vice President,
Bayer CropScience

At Bayer CropScience, we are proud to be an active corporate member of the Kansas City community, supplying the agriculture community around the world with novel products to protect the quality of our lives and our food.

Since our establishment in 1956, Bayer and our state have grown and changed in remarkable ways. Today, the Bayer CropScience Core Technology Center—based in Kansas City—contributes to the greater metropolitan area as a major employer of more than 800 highly skilled and dedicated employees.

Then as now, the spirit of innovation and enterprise invigorates Bayer CropScience as it does our great state.

This page, left: Busch Stadium, the current home of the St. Louis Cardinals, opened to much fanfare in 1966. Momentum is gathering again as enthusiasts await the opening of the Cardinals' new ballpark in 2006. Opposite page, right: The Kansas City Royals began playing in 1969, after the Kansas City Athletics moved to Oakland, California. Today, the Royals have a loyal following—tickets were sold out for the 2004 season opening-day game.

20-plus years, and the Kansas City Chiefs, who won the American Football Conference, western division, in 2003. The state's two professional baseball teams, the Kansas City Royals and the St. Louis Cardinals, are both World Series veterans. In St. Louis, fans are anticipating the 2006 opening of a new Cardinals ballpark, which will have sweeping views of the Gateway Arch and city skyline. A downtown revitalization will accompany the new stadium, with urban homes, restaurants, retailers, a public plaza, and a team museum.

MISSOURI PLAYGROUNDS

Forest blankets more than 14 million acres in Missouri, which makes the state seventh out of 20 northeastern states in the amount of forested acreage. Trees tantalize people outdoors, where they, along with snow egrets, barn owls, and northern harriers, bask in the state's flowing streams and rivers, limestone bluffs, endless prairies, and green hills.

Each year, about 18 million people visit the state park system, contributing $538 million annually to Missouri's economy. One of the state's best-known parks is the Katy Trail State Park, which traverses prairies, pastures, rolling hills, bluffs, river bottoms, wetlands, dense forests, and vineyards. In 1986, the Missouri-Kansas-Texas Railroad, nicknamed Katy, ceased operations between Sedalia and St. Charles. The state acquired the lonely corridor and revived it into a

Above: Some of the best rock climbing in the Midwest can be found in southern Missouri. Five state parks offer opportunities for climbing and rappelling. Opposite page, top: Iceskating is a winter tradition at Steinberg Skating Rink in St. Louis's Forest Park. Opposite page, bottom: Trout fishermen have cast their lines at Bennett Spring State Park in Lebanon since the early 1900s.

scenic bicycle and hiking trail spanning more than 200 miles across the state. Bird-watchers delight in sightings of orioles, chickadees, woodpeckers, robins, and bald eagles. The path wanders through rural towns hosting annual events such as the Big Muddy Folk Festival in Boonville, Scott Joplin Ragtime Festival in Sedalia, Pumpkin Festival in Hartsburg, and Lewis and Clark Rendezvous in Rocheport.

At the Lake of the Ozarks in central Missouri, opportunities flourish for fishing, hiking, camping, rock climbing, boating, waterskiing, cycling, canoeing, swimming, and skating (ice and otherwise). The lake encompasses 1,300 miles of shoreline, more than the California coast. Spelunkers find fun in the state's 5,500 caves,

earning Missouri another nickname, "The Cave State."

Recreational options exist in cities, too. Forest Park in St. Louis, which is bigger than New York's

Central Park, has pathways, waterways, and more. It is also a place of history. In 1904, the world descended upon the park to commemorate the centennial of the Lewis and Clark expedition and to watch the Summer Olympics, the first games on U.S. soil. The St. Louis World's Fair, as it was known, attracted 20 million visitors eager to see the latest technological advances and inventions. The eight-month event inspired the popular song, "Meet Me in St. Louis," an upbeat tune that catapulted Missouri into the international consciousness.

A century later, Missouri again celebrates Lewis and Clark, whose expedition launched 200 years—and counting—of discoveries.

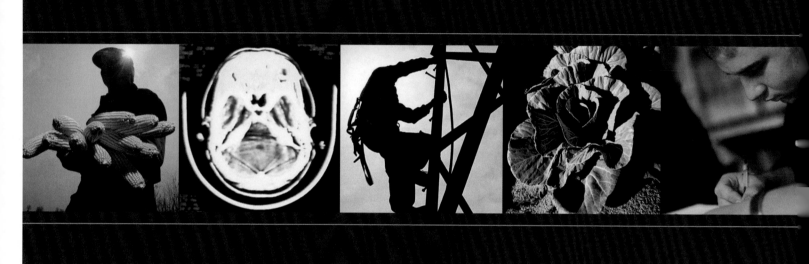

PART TWO

CHANGING THE WORLD

Missouri's Entrepreneurs and Innovators

FERTILE BEGINNINGS, A BOUNTIFUL FUTURE

Agriculture, Food Processing, Mining, and Forestry

Missouri's natural gifts have inspired generations of people. Its rich soil allows farmers to cultivate the region. Nurseries and crops of soybeans, wheat, rice, sorghum, and hay have arisen from the ground, feeding billions of dollars into the state's economy. Livestock become plump off the land, making Missouri a leader in cow, turkey, and hog production. Missouri's bounty also attracts leading food processing companies, which contribute to the well-being of people and animals around the world. Timber harvesters thrive with the state's nearly 14 million acres of forest, while miners flock to its ore-rich land.

A Growing Industry

One of Missouri's oldest companies began with a man lugging a saddlebag of apple scions in the wilds along the Mississippi River. In 1816, James Hart Stark headed west from Kentucky into the lush land that would become incorporated into the state of Missouri in 1821. There, in what is today Louisiana, Missouri, a small river town near the Illinois border, Stark grafted his family's apple tree shoots, sowing seeds of the now-famous Stark Bro's Nurseries &

Above: Missouri ranks sixth in the nation for soybean production. Shown is a farm near Keytesville. **Left:** Wine was first made in Missouri more than 150 years ago, and today, the state is home to nearly 30 wineries.

Orchards Company. From the nursery came some of the country's most popular apples—the Stark Red Delicious in 1893 and the Stark Golden Delicious in 1914. Today, the nursery runs a mail-order business and ships an estimated million trees a year, including apricot, persimmon, English walnut, and its patented quick-bearing tree, the Kwik Krop Fruit Tree.

Missouri inspired another nursery to establish roots, this time in 1949, in Elsberry, 50 miles north of St. Louis. Forrest Keeling Nursery started with a few evergreens in a backyard, hobby fodder for founder Hugh A. Steavenson and his father-in-law, Forrest Keeling. Their green thumbs turned a leisure activity into a business operating on 1,000 acres and growing more than four million

bare-root and container plants for wholesale markets worldwide. The nursery boasts an international reputation for research and has a well-known patented root propagation system that creates dense and fibrous roots that absorb more oxygen,

water, and nutrients than greenery grown conventionally.

Livestock companies also flourish in Missouri. Headquartered in Kansas City, Premium Standard Farms produces an estimated 135,000 sows in Missouri and Texas, distinguishing it

This page, top: Once a small business, Forrest Keeling Nursery in Elsberry has grown into a wholesale powerhouse. Shown is the company's garden center, circa 1970. This page, bottom: Evergreens are among the finished trees that Forrest Keeling Nursery offers. Opposite page: Hog production is a multimillion-dollar industry in Missouri.

as the nation's second largest pork producer. Businessmen Dennis Harms and Tad Gordon founded the company in 1988 with the objective to control all aspects of the operation, including farms, mills, and processing. The business set an industry standard in 2000 when it became the first in the country to install a carbon dioxide stunning system. Advocates believe the method is a humane way to anesthetize hogs and results in a higher quality of meat. Premium Standard Farms, which ships pork to more than 20 countries, had net sales of $608.4 million in fiscal 2003.

RECIPE FOR SUCCESS

Adolphus Busch dreamed of a national beer market when he began working at the St. Louis brewery that his father-in-law, Eberhard Anheuser, bought in 1860. In 1876, four years before Busch became president of Anheuser-Busch, he helped to introduce Budweiser, a light-hued lager that today outsells all of its competitors. In the 1870s, Busch pioneered using pasteurization methods for beer. He launched the industry's first fleet of refrigerated freight cars in 1881, and 15 years later, Michelob made its debut, eventually becoming the country's most popular super-premium beer. Successive Busch family members continued the legacy of innovation. August Busch, Adolphus Busch's son, kept business bubbling during Prohibition by

selling refrigeration units, syrup, soda, yeast, and other nonalcoholic products. August Busch III assumed leadership in 1975, launching a 27-year reign in which the company introduced its beer overseas, developed new products, delved into the theme park business, and created catchy commercials famous for Super Bowl Sunday debuts. In 2002, company veteran Patrick Stokes became the first non-Busch to head the company. A few months later, the company introduced the first low-carbohydrate beer, Michelob Ultra. More than a century of innovations turned a small, struggling brewery into the world's largest, and today, the company makes more than 30 beers and nonalcoholic drinks that are sold in more than 80 countries. Gross sales in 2003

topped $13.3 billion, and domestic beer sales volume set a record high.

Missouri boasts successful wineries as well. In 1965, when Jim and Betty Held bought Stone Hill Winery in Hermann, it was a flailing business. Established in 1847, the winery was once the third largest in the world and had won gold medals at eight World's Fairs. The Helds wanted to revive Stone Hill Winery's prestige. They went underground to the winery's series of vaulted cellars, removed mushrooms that had been growing inside, and restored the arched cellars, the nation's largest. The winery has since become the state's largest and most awarded.

Not all Missouri food processing companies cater to adults—the nation's second largest baby food producer, Beech-Nut Nutrition Corporation, is headquartered in St. Louis. The company's innovations stem from its philosophy to help infant growth and development. In 2002, it garnered attention by being the first baby food company to add docosahexaenoic acid (DHA) and arachidonic acid (ARA) to its food

Above: August Busch kept Anheuser-Busch in St. Louis afloat during Prohibition by selling nonalcoholic drinks such as ginger ale and root beer. Opposite page, top: Budweiser was available again in 1933, after beer was re-legalized. Shown is a 1929 billboard in New York City. Opposite page, bottom: In the early 1990s, the signature Budweiser brand was joined by Bud Dry, Ice Draft from Budweiser, and Ice Draft Light from Budweiser.

Beech-Nut STRAINED FOODS

SOUPS · FRUITS · VEGETABLES · CEREALS

IN STERILIZED GLASS JARS

All the good in nature prepared with
All the care of BEECH-NUT
for babies everywhere

unnecessary additives such as salt in 1977, chemically modified starch in 1985, and refined sugar in 1997. Through a series of mergers, the company relocated its baby food headquarters to St. Louis in 1989. Part of the Milnot Company, Beech-Nut Nutrition Corporation sells more than 100 products, including baby food, juices, cereals, and microwaveable meals for toddlers.

Nestle Purina PetCare Company, another Missouri food processing business, was founded based on the philosophy that "Animals must eat year-round." This was Missourian William H. Danforth's conclusion in 1892, and two years later, he started a business in St. Louis mixing formula feeds for farm animals. Danforth's dedication transformed the small business into Ralston Purina, one of the country's most successful animal care companies. A former farm boy with health problems, Danforth believed in balancing mental and physical health and expressed this philosophy as a checkerboard pattern on his packaging. His distinctive trademark was revolutionary—few businesses used logos and sales promotions at the time. In 2001, the company merged with a Nestle subsidiary, forming Nestle Purina PetCare Company. The St. Louis–based firm is the world's largest producer of dry dog food and soft cat food.

under the Beech-Nut First Advantage line. These fatty acids, which occur naturally in breast milk, can help to improve a baby's mental and visual development.

The company's heritage goes back to 1891, when Raymond and Walter Lipe, David Zieley, and Bartlett Arkell decided to join the meat-packaging industry in Canajoharie, New York, as Imperial Packing Company. Its operations quickly expanded, and by 1931 it was producing baby food. Beech-Nut Nutrition Corporation was the first company to put baby food in glass jars instead of lead-soldered metal cans, and it was the first to offer a complete baby food line banning

LAND OF PLENTY

T. W. Boswell saw a future in white oak trees dotting Missouri's landscape. In 1912, he founded Independent Stave Company, based in Lebanon, Missouri, to supply thin, shaped wood strips to barrel makers. Not long after the company was founded, however, Prohibition caused many cooperages, distillers, and wineries to close. Later, the beer industry's switch to stainless steel vats made matters worse. But Independent Stave Company survived and thrived when it started producing white oak barrels for bourbon and whiskey in the early 1950s. In 1976, the company began providing barrels for the wine industry. Today, the Boswell family owns and operates five stave and heading mills, including operations

in France and Bulgaria. They also oversee 15 log yards throughout the Midwest. Independent Stave Company is the world's largest barrel maker, marketing its products to 19 countries.

Doe Run Company, the world's largest primary lead producer, found its calling beneath southern Missouri's rolling hills. It evolved from the St. Joseph Lead Company, which bought acres of Missouri's ore-rich land in the 1860s. Back then, miners dug trenches eight feet

Above: In the 19th century, miners chiseled away at soil with pickaxes. Shown are Missouri lead miners, circa 1890. Opposite page, top: Recycling programs reduce waste by staggering amounts each year. Opposite page, bottom: Smelting is a carefully calibrated process.

deep, milled soil with pickaxes, and used charcoal ovens for smelter. In 1923, St. Joseph Lead Company invented the roof bolt to secure overhead rock, which is still an industry standard. Today, locating and extracting the mineral occurs about 1,000 feet belowground with more sophisticated equipment the company has developed throughout the years. Doe Run Company's seven mines in Missouri provide 70 percent of the nation's primary lead supply. The St. Louis–based company uses state-of-the-art technology in its mines, mills, smelters, and lead fabrication plants in Missouri, Washington, Arizona, Texas, and Peru. Workers also process gold, silver, zinc, and copper. In 2002, Doe Run Company's Mining and Milling Division extracted an estimated five million tons of ore.

Full Circle

The state's generous natural resources encourage industries to give back to the land. Anheuser-Busch runs the world's largest recycling operation for aluminum beverage containers, recycling nearly 754 million pounds in 2003. Overall, the company recycles more than 97 percent of the waste it generates through composting, packaging-reduction programs, and other methods. Doe Run Company's concern for the land translated into its development of the world's largest recycling lead smelter, which reduced total waste by 239,000 tons in 2002.

Premium Standard Farms converts animal waste into nutrient-rich, organic fertilizer. Independent Stave Company created Missouri Mulch in 1995, a subsidiary to harvest by-products into landscape materials. This allows the company to use nearly 100 percent of the white oak trees they harvest. Forrest Keeling Nursery works with conservationists in implementing its root production systems in wetland and reforestation projects, increasing plant survival rates roughly 85 percent. The symbiotic relationship between Missouri and its industries shows no sign of abating.

A LEGACY OF LEARNING
Education

Early educators were eager to build Missouri into an intellectual warehouse where ideas, inventions, and innovations thrived. Released from the restraints of established East Coast institutions, knowledge-seekers delighted in their freedom to pursue scholarly interests. They forged top law schools that succeeded, in part, because they had the foresight to include women and minorities in their programs. Journalism found a home in Missouri, both at the world's first school for the profession and at one of the nation's oldest college newspapers. African-American soldiers opened the Midwest's first learning institution for freed slaves, and a local doctor established the first school of osteopathic medicine. Today, one college even offers students a tuition-free degree. That is how important education is in Missouri.

BROADENING THE MIND

Attracted to Missouri's frontier, Reverend Louis William Du Bourg, once the Catholic bishop of Louisiana, moved to St. Louis and opened St. Louis College in 1818. The school struggled until 1826,

Above: Lincoln University in Jefferson City, shown circa 1900, set a precedent in the late 1860s by dedicating itself to educating freed slaves. Today, the university's students come from a variety of ethnic backgrounds. Left: More than 360,000 students are enrolled at Missouri's higher education institutions.

when Du Bourg asked the Society of Jesus, or the Jesuits, to take over the college. The Jesuits agreed, eager to promulgate the teachings of St. Ignatius Loyola, who wanted young people to learn how to become spiritual, practical, and socially responsible adults. In 1832, with the state's blessing, the school received a formal charter as Saint Louis University, making it the oldest university west of the Mississippi River and the nation's second Jesuit-run institution of higher education. Saint Louis University established the region's first graduate school in 1832, one of the country's oldest law schools in 1843, and the Western Hemisphere's first department of geophysics in 1925. The oldest federally licensed aviation institution, Parks Air College in St. Louis, became affiliated with the university in 1946. During the 1980s, the university began transforming blight into beauty in surrounding neighborhoods by refurbishing old buildings and encouraging businesses to invest in the area. Saint Louis University's reputation attracts students from all 50 states and 90 foreign countries, with more than 11,200 students enrolled for the 2002–2003 academic year.

The oldest state college west of the Mississippi River was inspired by Thomas Jefferson's push for public higher education. The University of Missouri System was established in

Columbia in 1839, and in 1870, the university assumed land-grant status, encouraging the Missouri legislature to approve a college of agriculture and mechanical arts. That same year, the legislature authorized a new campus in Rolla, where a school of mines and metallurgy was established. In 1908, Walter Williams, a newspaper editor from Boonville, founded the world's first journalism school at the Columbia campus. Williams believed that students wishing to pursue journalism and advertising careers needed special, hands-on training. The school continues to rank as one of the best in the world. Columbia was also the site for another first, this time in 1917, when it conducted soil erosion experiments that served as the core of the U.S. Soil Conservation Service's erosion reduction program. In 1963, campuses were established in Kansas City and St. Louis. Today, more than 50,000 students attend the University of Missouri System, making it one of the nation's 20 largest higher learning institutions.

Journalism, along with other academic subjects, found another home at Washington University in St. Louis. Originally founded in 1853 as Eliot Seminary, the university distinguished itself early on. In 1869, its law school was one of the first in the nation to admit women. Today, about 40 percent of Washington University's law school students are women. Another first occurred in 1878, when the university's independent newspaper, *Student Life,* hit newsstands almost a year before the region's main newspaper, the *St. Louis Post-Dispatch.* *Student Life* is now one of the country's oldest college papers. Washington University is also known for its stellar schools of architecture, arts, and engineering and applied science, the latter of which includes faculty who have received more than 130 patents.

The university's schools of medicine and business have secured its reputation as the "Ivy League of the Midwest," attracting top scholars from around the world. Washington University has approximately 13,600 students and offers more than 90 study programs.

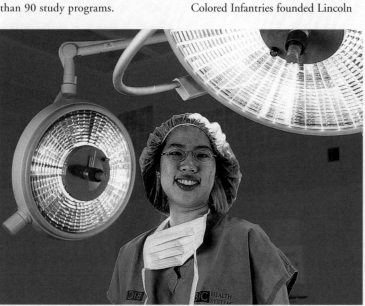

OPENING OPPORTUNITIES

As the Civil War ended, Missouri's African-American soldiers wanted a learning institution that would emphasize the educational and social needs of freed slaves. With $6,400, enlisted men in the 62nd and 65th Colored Infantries founded Lincoln

Institute in Jefferson City in 1866 to help African-Americans succeed in education and labor. The first of its kind in the Midwest, the school began receiving state aid for teacher training in 1870. Seven years later, Lincoln Institute offered college-level studies. In 1879, it became a state institution, and 11 years later, Lincoln Institute received land-grant status, prompting school officials to add industrial and agricultural courses to the curriculum. In 1921, the institute changed its name to Lincoln University, and during the next 13 years, the university received state accreditation for various programs. Lincoln University diversified its student population in 1954, under the U.S. Supreme Court ruling *Brown v. Board of Education,* but its core mission to prepare students for

Above: Memorial Tower at the University of Missouri–Columbia, shown in the 1930s, stands about 140 feet tall. Made of limestone, the building is part of the university's "white campus;" brick buildings define "red campus." Opposite page, top: Groundbreaking scientific research conducted at Washington University in St. Louis has earned it an enviable reputation. Opposite page, bottom: Admission to Washington University's School of Medicine is highly competitive—there are usually more than 30 applicants for each open spot.

Above: Although more than 11,000 students attend Saint Louis University, the school boasts a 13-to-1 student-to-teacher ratio. Opposite page, top: Lincoln University, which resurrected its football program in 1999, also has basketball, softball, and track-and-field programs. Opposite page, bottom: The University of Missouri–Columbia's Tigers football team has a loyal following. Shown is a home game at Memorial Stadium in the late 1940s.

college, which in 1967 graduated its first class. The four-year, liberal arts college emphasizes hard work and education, requiring its 1,500 students to earn tuition by working on campus 15 hours a week, plus occasional 40-hour workweeks. The school is one of a handful of such colleges in the nation. Students toil toward their degrees while also constructing academic buildings, landscaping grounds, working in cafeterias, milking cows, operating a campus fire station, and growing orchids for one of the largest orchid collections on any campus in the United States. The goal is to enrich learning, instill a solid work ethic, and provide students who may not

prosperity remained. Today, more than 3,100 students attend the university.

Educational access is the founding principle of another Missouri school, College of the Ozarks in Point Lookout, where tuition is free.

Established in 1906 by James Forsythe, a Presbyterian minister, the school started as a campus to teach elementary and high school students from low-income families. The program expanded to include a

be able to afford college a chance to earn degrees. The college's graduates have a job placement rate of more than 99 percent.

BODY OF KNOWLEDGE

Andrew Taylor Still dismissed most drugs, convinced that they failed to fight most diseases. Instead, the experienced doctor believed the human body could heal itself. The trick was to detect and correct anatomical abnormalities that obstructed blood's free flow. He focused on the musculo-skeletal system, an interconnected highway of muscles, bones, and nerves that comprises about two-thirds of the body. Still's medical philosophy created osteopathy in 1885. Seven years later, Still founded what is known today as the Kirksville College of Osteopathic Medicine in Kirksville, the nation's first school

devoted to the emerging field. The college started in a two-frame building, with the first class graduating in 1894. Still's push for holistic treatment continues today at the four-year school, which has an enrollment of about 600 students.

STEPPING-STONES TO SUCCESS

Missouri's largest junior college system, the St. Louis Community College System, was created by the state's general assembly in 1961 and approved by voters one year later.

Like other junior college districts during the 1960s, the St. Louis system was spurred in response to the passage of the Higher Education Act in 1965, which guaranteed federal help to students demonstrating financial need. That same year, St. Louis voters overwhelmingly approved a $47.2 million bond issue to build three campuses—the country's most ambitious construction program for junior college development at the time. In 1966, the district received national accolades for designing the school system on computers, saving space and $3 million. In 1971, the St. Louis system opened its Child Development Center, a nationally renowned educational laboratory and demonstration facility used to tend to infants and toddlers, and to train students interested in pursuing careers in child care. The site was the first of its kind at a community college. Today, the St. Louis Community College System serves 26,000 students within 700 square miles of its three campuses.

Picture of Dr Still

Above: Dr. Andrew Taylor Still, founder of the Kirksville College of Osteopathic Medicine in Kirksville, shook up mainstream medicine with his holistic approach to healing. Opposite page, top: Preschools across the country have been influenced by the St. Louis Community College System's Child Development Center, which has served as a national model. Opposite page, bottom: In 2003, students from more than 30 countries came to Missouri's higher education institutions to earn bachelor's degrees.

BUILDING ASSETS
Finance, Insurance, Real Estate, and Construction

The Show-Me State presents an impressive portfolio to entrepreneurs, offering a wealth of opportunities with the continuity, diversity, and resources ideal for a smart investment. During the 19th and 20th centuries, innovators established reputable financial institutions in Missouri. They protected the property and possessions of homeowners and farmers. They developed communities,

structures, and entertainment centers. People continue to flock to the state today, realizing that hard work pays dividends in the form of world-class cities and a comfortable lifestyle.

Money Matters

Edward Jones's success hinges on thinking small. The St. Louis–based brokerage firm courts average-income families, unlike most major Wall Street

firms that prefer customers with accounts over $100,000. Edward Jones shuns posh offices brimming with big-city brokers. Instead, it insists that financial planners set up one-person shops, often in far-flung locations across the country and the world. At Edward Jones, a high-rise office usually means the second floor of a brick building on a rural Main Street or the third story of an urban strip mall.

Above: The Missouri Department of Economic Development can help local developers to access a number of incentive programs, including grants and tax credits. Left: Nearly 2,000 personal financial advisors worked in Missouri in 2002.

The company traces its roots to Whitaker & Co., a traditional bond house founded in 1871. Edward D. Jones Sr. established his namesake brokerage in 1922 and 21 years later, merged with Whitaker & Co. It was not until 1955, however, that the company's counterintuitive philosophy took hold. Edward D. "Ted" Jones Jr. found a niche in underserved rural communities, where local brokers and their neighbors could have face-to-face meetings. That year, Ted Jones Jr. opened the firm's first branch office in the town of Mexico, Missouri. Today, Edward Jones boasts about 8,000 offices nationwide, more than many other U.S. brokerages. The company plans to open 25,000 more offices in the next decade. Its sales in 2002 were anything but small: $2.2 billion.

Community is the focus of Commerce Bank as well. Unlike most banks, where people become numbers and sometimes get charged for banking in person, Commerce Bank has a humanistic approach. Its employees have received training in mom-and-pop customer service. This personal style goes back to 1865, when the bank's founder, Francis Reid Long, invested $10,000 in a small, customer-friendly savings association in Kansas City. By listening to customer needs, the company grew into a national bank in 1890. Commerce Bank also became an industry leader in technology. In 1928, it started the country's first 24-hour transit department. In 1984, the bank was the first to offer a card that functioned as a credit and ATM card.

Above and opposite page, bottom: From its beginning as a single bank in Kansas City, Commerce Bank has grown into a banking powerhouse, with more than 330 locations in three states. On this page, a lobby is shown in the 1920s; on the opposite page, a lobby in the 1950s. Opposite page, top: A technological leader, Commerce Bank was the first U.S. bank to offer a card that could be used as an ATM and credit card.

Today, Commerce Bank is one of the nation's largest banking chains, with headquarters in Kansas City and St. Louis, more than 330 operations extending into Kansas and Illinois, and assets of $13.4 billion.

DOLLARS AND SENSE

The Bloch brothers envisioned starting a small financial business in Kansas City, their hometown. Armed with a university degree and military service, Henry Bloch borrowed $5,000 from his aunt during the mid-1900s. He used the money to start a bookkeeping company in a rented, $50-a-month storeroom office on Main Street. In 1955, about the time the Internal Revenue Service stopped doing people's income taxes for free, Henry and his brother Richard formed H&R Block, a firm specializing in income tax

return preparation. A year later, the company established offices in New York and in 1957, opened franchises nationwide. As technology advanced, H&R Block soared to the forefront of filing tax returns electronically, which allowed taxpayers to receive refunds faster, leading to the company's trademarked "Rapid Refund." In

2000, financial operations expanded to include brokerage services, mutual funds, and IRAs. Through the years, the company has expanded from a single workroom to 10,000 tax offices worldwide and nearly 100 financial centers nationwide. H&R Block, whose headquarters remain in Kansas City, prepares tax returns for more than 18 million people each year. The company reported revenues of $3.8 billion in 2003.

SAFEGUARDING PEOPLE AND PROPERTY

Shelter Insurance in Columbia owes its beginnings to a cooperative of Missouri farmers needing affordable automobile coverage. In 1946, the farmers were impressed because Shelter Insurance offered attractive rates, and, as a mutual insurance company, the opportunity for members to be partial owners. The farmers' backing—along

shopping center designed for auto-mobile drivers. It was a postwar pro-totype for the modern mall. He modeled the marketplace after those found in Spain, incorporating pastel buildings, red-tiled roofs, airy courtyards, bubbling fountains, bright tile work, and a 130-foot tower inspired by the Giralda Tower at the Great Cathedral in Seville, Spain. Today, Country Club Plaza stretches 14 blocks, luring locals and out-of-towners to dine at fine restau-rants, listen to live music, and shop at more than 120 stores. Artwork and sculptures adorn the property.

Around the same time the Country Club Plaza was being built, AMC Entertainment premiered with the opening of a movie theater in Kansas City. Its operations were directed by a newly married Edward Durwood, whose credits included running tent shows throughout the

with competitive rates and reputable customer service—accelerated Shelter Insurance's growth. The company grew into an industry leader in technology, embracing state-of-the-art computer programs that allow its 1,400 licensed agents to customize databases about potential clients. Shelter Insurance operates in 13 states and brought in $1 billion in premiums in 2003.

REVOLUTIONS IN REAL ESTATE
In 1903, a swollen Kansas River swallowed humans and homes, devas-tating parts of Kansas City. Jesse Clyde Nichols, who would become one of the country's most influential real estate developers, marked the beginning of his career by building and selling houses for some of the 20,000 people left homeless by the flood. That experience helped to

shape his philosophy in urban planning. Nichols looked beyond basic house construction. He created communities intertwining people's cultural, religious, social, and retail needs. He considered the rising pop-ularity of autos. In 1922, Nichols built the Country Club Plaza in Kansas City, the nation's first

H&R BLOCK

world headquarters

Above: In 2006, H&R Block will move its current Kansas City headquarters from this building to another location in downtown Kansas City. The new, 500,000-square-foot building will be a key piece of a downtown revitalization project. Opposite page, top: About 87 percent of H&R Block's clients received refunds in 2003. Opposite page, bottom: In addition to auto insurance, Shelter Insurance in Columbia offers homeowner's, life, business, and farm owner's insurance.

Above and opposite page, bottom: Generations of people have enjoyed Country Club Plaza in Kansas City, the unique vision of developer Jesse Clyde Nichols. Like Kansas City itself, the plaza is filled with fountains. Opposite page, top: Kansas City–based AMC Entertainment has theaters around the world, including this one in New York City's Times Square.

Midwest. By the 1950s, the business, Durwood Theatres, operated about a dozen theaters and drive-ins. However, it was Durwood's son, Stanley Durwood, a Harvard graduate and army lieutenant, who became company president in 1960 and projected big ideas for the theater chain. In 1963, he introduced the country's first multiple-screen movie theater at a mall in Kansas City. During the 1960s, business expanded westward into other states, including California, the entertainment industry's hub. With 68 screens nationwide, the chain changed its name to American Multi-Cinema in 1968 and shortened it to AMC 15 years later. In 1981, the company patented the popular cup-holder armrest. AMC Entertainment introduced stadium seating in 1995 and created MovieTickets.com, a Web site selling tickets, in 2000. Today, the Kansas City–based company ranks as the nation's second largest movie theater chain, with 3,500 screens in the United States, Canada, Europe, and Asia.

BUILDING THE STATE

In 1985, when Greg Walton established his construction company in Kansas City, he applied proven business principles such as quality customer service, materials, and craftsmanship. What distinguishes Walton Construction Company as one of the country's top contractors, however, is its emphasis on advanced technology, specifically construction software. The firm's high-tech infrastructure garnered industry accolades for allowing the company to continue its renovation of the Kansas City International Airport following the September 11, 2001, terrorist attacks. The lead contractor for the $229 million, four-year airport-terminal improvement project, Walton Construction Company had just begun construction when the tragedy occurred. The firm

immediately halted plans on its $100 million contract and relied on its computer technology to modify blueprints, implement new security procedures, and regularly alert 35 subcontractors about changing aviation standards. Because of its technological innovations, Walton Construction Company averted costly delays in renovating the airport's three 1970s-era terminals, where improvements are scheduled to be completed in 2004.

SHARING THE WEALTH

Missouri's successful financial, insurance, real estate, and construction companies believe philanthropy is an essential investment. For more than 25 years, H&R Block has contributed more than $18 million in grants to ballets, schools, mental health facilities, children's theater, and other organizations to improve metropolitan Kansas City. Walton Construction Company also contributes financially to charities, in addition to lending carpenters to help build homes for Habitat for Humanity. While Shelter Insurance distributes hundreds of thousands of dollars in scholarships, it also offers a free garden in Columbia with more than 300 trees and shrubs and 15,000 annuals and perennials. AMC Entertainment encourages children to read during the summer with an incentive program that offers free soda and popcorn for every three books completed. Approximately 800,000 children have read more than two million publications since the program started in 1989. Such acts will yield compound returns in Missouri's future.

Above: Walton Construction Company in Kansas City often lends carpenters to Habitat for Humanity. Opposite page, top: As part of the construction of Bartle Hall in Kansas City, Walton Construction Company had to install four massive, 300-foot pylons. The pylons help to support a building that stretches across a freeway. Opposite page, bottom: The construction industry in Missouri employed more than 15,000 laborers in 2002.

MODERN MEDICINE
Health Care and Biotechnology

Missourians have long believed that the health of the region depends on the wellness of its people. During the 1800s, newcomers nursed the sick during outbreaks of smallpox, the flu, and other maladies. Missouri's medical minds expanded as research centers and schools made curing, soothing, and preventing illness a regional priority. Today, the state takes pride in having some of the nation's best hospitals, attracting doctors and scientists who are leaders in their specialties. Missouri also dominates in biotechnology and plant science. In 2003, the Danforth Foundation, a philanthropic group, announced it would give $117 million during two years to transform the St. Louis area into a Silicon Valley for the country's ascending biotech and plant sciences sector.

Aiding the Ailing

On November 16, 1872, five nuns fleeing religious persecution in Germany arrived in St. Louis with $5 among them and a desire to help the needy. The next day, they cared for smallpox patients. The nuns, whose convent was near St. Mary's Church, soon became known as the Sisters of St. Mary. In 1877, they established their first hospital,

Above: There are more than 60 hospitals in Missouri, about half of which are in St. Louis and Kansas City. People throughout the state, however, need not look far for medical care, including emergency services. Left: In 2002, Missouri's health care industry employed 218,000 people.

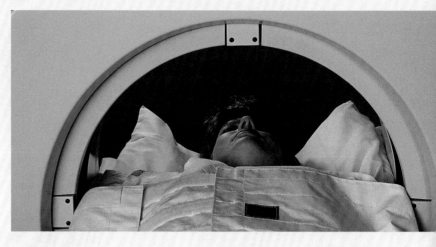

St. Mary's Infirmary near downtown St. Louis. During the 1960s, the nuns started a detoxification center, a clinic for migrant workers, and mobile facilities for low-income pregnant women. Their growing health care regime culminated in the SSM Health Care System in 1986. One of the nation's largest Catholic systems, the St. Louis–based non-profit owns, operates, and is affiliated with 21 acute care hospitals, including nine in Missouri. With facilities in four states, SSM Health Care System also runs nursing homes, rehabilitation clinics, pediatric care centers, hospices, home health agencies, physician practices, and more.

The Sisters of Mercy Health System in St. Louis also traces its roots to a group of nuns. In 1871, the Sisters of Mercy converted a

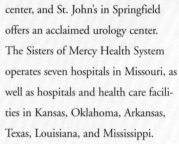

St. Louis schoolroom into an infirmary for women and children. By 1873, the infirmary had become a general hospital called St. John's. The sisters established Springfield's first hospital in 1891 and continued to open hospitals in other states in the following years. Today, St. John's Mercy Medical Center in St. Louis offers a broad spectrum of services, including the state's largest burn

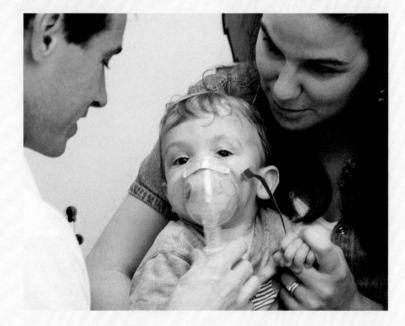

center, and St. John's in Springfield offers an acclaimed urology center. The Sisters of Mercy Health System operates seven hospitals in Missouri, as well as hospitals and health care facilities in Kansas, Oklahoma, Arkansas, Texas, Louisiana, and Mississippi.

St. Louis is also home to Washington University, which founded its School of Medicine in 1891 to improve doctors' training. Today, that mission perseveres, with its faculty and students working at the renowned Barnes-Jewish Hospital and St. Louis Children's Hospital.

In 1909, Robert Brookings, a businessman and philanthropist, decided to transform the medical school into one of the country's best by modernizing it, adding laboratories, and attracting endowments and a full-time faculty. His recruits included a Nobel Prize winner and a surgeon who, in 1933, became the first to remove a lung successfully. Many other medical firsts occurred at

Washington University, catapulting the School of Medicine's reputation. During the early 1970s, the school introduced the first positron emission tomography (PET) scanner, used to image the brain. Researchers also discovered that taking aspirin could prevent heart attacks. In 1990, Washington University scientists found a cure for hepatitis B. A year later, a doctor invented a blood test for early diagnosis of prostate cancer. The medical school's resume of firsts also includes creating a rating scale

that diagnoses Alzheimer's disease and a genetic test that detects whether a person will develop a form of thyroid cancer. The university's ongoing research highlights esteemed projects in genetics, nerve transplant, surgical techniques, and drug therapies.

The School of Medicine's faculty and students practice and train at medical facilities run by BJC HealthCare, one of the largest nonprofit health care organizations in the country, with almost 26,000 employees and net revenues of $2.4 billion in 2002.

Barnes-Jewish Hospital, BJC HealthCare's flagship hospital, is Missouri's largest, with 1,385 patient beds and more than 9,000 employees, including a medical staff of full-time Washington University faculty and private physicians. Patients from other states and countries seek treatment at the hospital, which is consistently ranked as one of the nation's best. As part of a 1996 expansion project, Barnes-Jewish Hospital also offers several niche facilities. Among them is the Center for Advanced Medicine,

Above: St. Louis Children's Hospital treats nearly 225,000 patients each year. Founded in 1879, it is the oldest pediatric hospital west of the Mississippi River. Opposite page, top: Patients continue to benefit from the PET scan technology invented 30 years ago by the Washington University School of Medicine in St. Louis. Opposite page, bottom: Parents can choose from a range of hospitals and clinics in Missouri for their children's care.

which houses 17 medical and surgical specialties for outpatient care.

Ill children from around the world turn to St. Louis Children's Hospital, which has more than 30 pediatric subspecialties and the highest level of emergency care available. The facility offers the world's largest pediatric lung transplant program and one of the best bone marrow transplant centers in the United States. Overall, it is one of the nation's top three pediatric transplant centers. Its vitae also includes one of the country's largest cochlear implant programs for patients with hearing impairments, an internationally acclaimed cerebral palsy center, and the esteemed Cleft Palate and Craniofacial Deformities Institute.

Better Health, One Rx at a Time

Express Scripts in Maryland Heights prides itself on delivering prescription drugs fast and cheap. It is one of the nation's largest pharmacy benefits management companies, with more than 50 million members in the United States and Canada. The business began in 1986 when

HMO Sanus teamed with Medicare-Glaser, with the idea that the St. Louis–based drugstore chain would manage Sanus's prescription program. Express Scripts grew to include mail-order options, vision services, and infusion therapy. In 1989, Medicare-Glaser went bankrupt and Sanus dissolved into New York Life, which today owns about 20 percent of the company. During the 1990s, Express Scripts expanded, and in 2002, the firm acquired National Prescription Administrators, the country's largest private pharmacy benefits manage-

ment company. Express Scripts buys directly from manufacturers, maintains relationships with retailers, negotiates hard, and avoids possible conflicts of interest stemming from ties to drug behemoths. Each year, the company processes more than 380 million prescriptions.

Pioneering Medicine

Brothers Edward, Otto, and Gustav Mallinckrodt knew there was more to medicine than expunging evil spirits from the body. In 1867, they formed G. Mallinckrodt & Company in St. Louis to develop

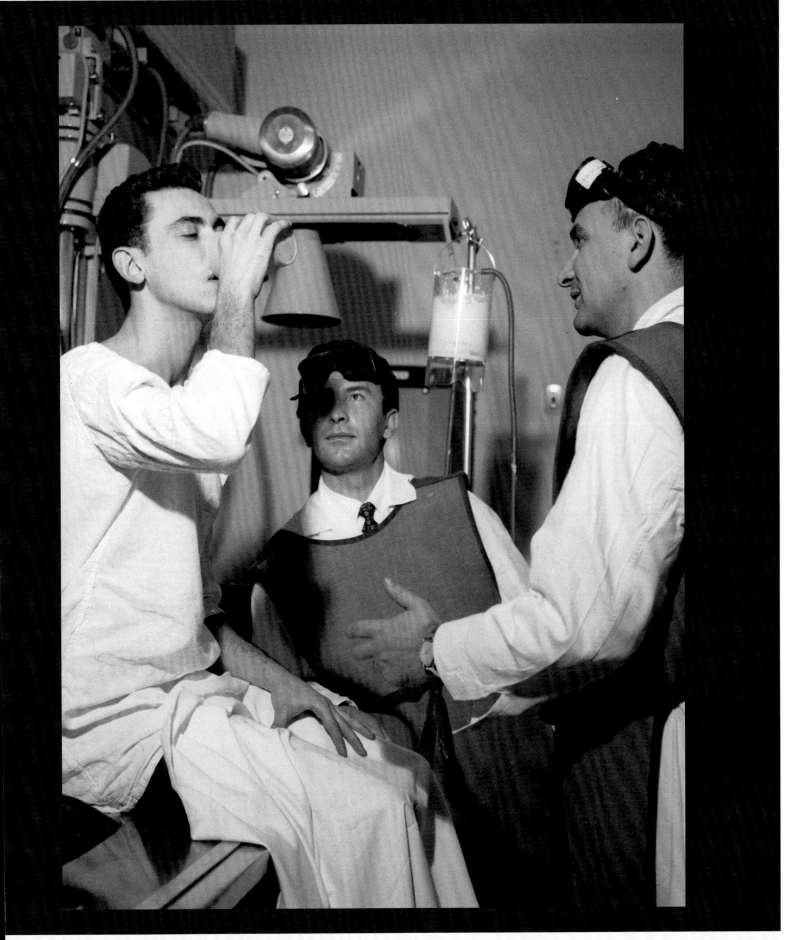

Above: Mallinckrodt in Hazelwood has produced barium sulfate products since its early days. Shown is a patient drinking barium sulfate before having an X ray taken in 1956. Opposite page, top (from left to right): Edward, Gustav, and Otto Mallinckrodt believed in the power of science. Opposite page, bottom: The Washington University School of Medicine, shown in the 1950s, has a long history of medical firsts.

Above: Tablet dissolution tests are part of the drug development process. Opposite page, top: Barnes-Jewish Hospital in St. Louis, which has the world's largest lung transplant program, is also recognized for robotic heart and beating heart surgery. Opposite page, bottom: Rather than undergo surgery, male puppies can be neutered with an injection created by Addison Biological Laboratory in Fayette.

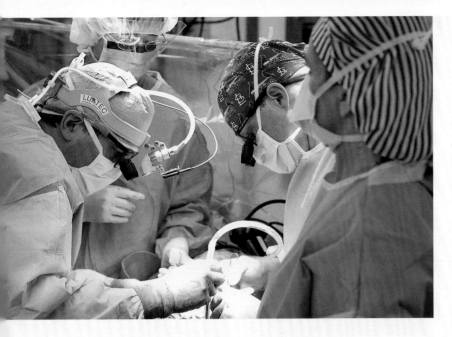

chemical remedies for fighting diseases, making it the only chemical maker west of Philadelphia at the time. During the company's first 40 years, Mallinckrodt became the top producer of anhydrous ammonia, a key substance for refrigeration. It created commercial barium sulfate, used in X-ray diagnosis. The company forayed into nuclear science during the 1940s, purifying uranium oxide, used in the world's first self-sustaining nuclear reactor. During the second half of the 20th century, Mallinckrodt became a leading supplier of specialty chemicals, health care goods, and food, flavor, and fragrance products. It also specialized in marketing and manufacturing biomedical lab equipment, radiopharmaceuticals, and catalysts. In 1999, the company introduced chemical products to help sleep apnea, attention deficit disorder, and narcolepsy. Tyco International bought the company in 2000, maintaining its headquarters

in Hazelwood. Today, Mallinckrodt operates in more than 100 countries and boasts about 35 global manufacturing facilities.

Improving the health of animals is

J. Bruce Addison's mission. His company, Addison Biological Laboratory in Fayette, is an esteemed manufacturer and marketer of veterinary technologies. In the mid-1970s, after six years of managing a veterinary lab at the University of Missouri–Columbia, Addison set off on his own, opening labs and studying ways to battle bacterial strains harmful to animals. His company incorporated in 1983. Addison's laboratory has created vaccines that fight intestinal disorders in cattle, sheep, and goats. Scientists have developed herd-specific vaccines

to treat a farmer's livestock. The laboratory has launched product lines that help to eliminate pinkeye in cattle and intranasal respiratory infections in baby pigs. Addison Biological Laboratory also offers items in animal dermatology, otology, and veterinary dental home care. In 2003, the laboratory began marketing a veterinary breakthrough—a chemical injection that neuters male puppies, allowing dogs to bypass surgical castration and possible complications. Addison Biological Laboratory exports its products to more than 25 countries.

EXPLORATIONS IN SCIENCE

International powerhouse Monsanto started as a seed when John Francis Queeny, a veteran in the pharmaceutical business, started a company catering to the pharmaceutical and food industries in 1901. More than a century later, the St. Louis–based company has grown into a leader in biotechnology crops. In 1902, the company began manufacturing saccharin, which it shipped exclusively to the Coca-Cola Company in Georgia between 1903 and 1905. During this time, Monsanto started offering chemical ingredients, caffeine, and vanillin. It also began aspirin production in 1917. Queeny's son, Edgar, credited for turning Monsanto into a worldwide industry leader, became president in 1928, with the

immediate goal of expanding the company to include rubber chemicals and phosphates. During World War II, Monsanto researched uranium for the Manhattan Project, a now-defunct U.S. agency responsible for developing the first atomic bombs. Following the war, Monsanto focused on manufacturing insecticides, herbicides, plastics, and synthetic fibers. Roundup emerged in 1974 and remains the world's best-selling herbicide. In 1982, for the first time in history, the company's scientists genetically modified a plant cell, leading to other innovations in growing plants with genetically engineered traits. In 1989, Monsanto spawned another success with the release of Cytotec, the world's first anti-ulcer medication. The 1990s echoed Monsanto's growth in biotechnology. It introduced medications to treat insomnia and arthritis. One of the world's top seed producers,

Monsanto had net sales of $4.9 billion in fiscal 2003.

FEELING PHILANTHROPIC, FEELING GOOD

Local health care, pharmaceutical, and biotechnology companies believe charity and volunteerism contribute to good health. In 2002, the Monsanto Fund, Monsanto's philanthropic arm, delivered $13.9 million in grants to support better crop yields, nutrition, education, and other charitable causes. That same year, SSM Health Care System gave $35 million in free services to the poor and an additional $44 million in unreimbursed costs under Medicaid. Each year, Mallinckrodt donates approximately $2 million to organizations that feed the hungry, offer children free dental clinics, and provide resource centers for health and human services.

Above and opposite page: Biotechnology companies such as Monsanto in St. Louis are delving into promising plant research. Above is a genetically engineered seedling being observed in a laboratory. Opposite is a farmer holding pink corn seed, which gets its unusual color from a chemical spray that protects it from pests and disease.

ON THE CUTTING EDGE

Information Technology, Communications, and the Media

Missouri's future beams, thanks in part to information technology companies whose digital pursuits benefit people living in all corners of the globe. Because of these businesses, North America's railcar systems run more efficiently, as do the country's financial institutions and the world's hospitals and medical offices. Millions of people nationwide also depend on Missouri's technology-savvy communications and media companies to keep them globally wired and well-informed. These growing industries ensure that the state will soar into the future.

HOOKED ON TECHNOLOGY

In 1976, Jack Henry and Jerry Hall fiddled with a borrowed computer behind an engine repair shop in Purdy, so much so that an idea sprang for a technological company catering to small financial institutions. They developed software systems for community banks, set up a workspace in the back of a tire shop in Monett, and in 1977, formed Jack Henry & Associates. Today, the company, with larger offices but still based in Monett, offers software and hardware that provide data processing, automated transactions,

---

Above and opposite page: The information technology industry, which ranges from computer software companies to computer service firms, is thriving in Missouri. In fact, this growing sector employs more than 70,000 Missourians and contributes billions of dollars to the state economy each year.

electronic funds transfers, automated teller machine (ATM) networking, and tools for Internet banking, among other technologies. Its services keep banks nationwide successful and competitive. The company also assists with computer maintenance. Jack Henry & Associates employs about 2,000 people and conducts business with more than 2,350 financial institutions, including credit unions. In fiscal 2003, the company's revenue exceeded $404 million.

Inspiration for another software company struck in 1979 at a picnic table at Loose Park in Kansas City, where three men decided that the health care industry needed state-of-the-art software programs. Founders Neal Patterson, Paul Gorup, and Cliff Illig incorporated PGI & Associates the following year. In 1984, the company changed its name to Cerner Corporation and

introduced its first product, PathNet, a laboratory information system, commercially. Throughout the 1980s and 1990s, the company offered software programs to manage medical records; automate clinical, financial, and administrative information; and connect emergency rooms to pharmacies and other departments. In response to the September 11, 2001, terrorist

attacks, Cerner Corporation, with the Kansas City Health Department, created an early warning computer system to notify medical workers about possible disease outbreaks and to track potential bioterrorist assaults. Today, the company has more than 1,500 clients and employs more than 5,100 people worldwide. Cerner Corporation's 2003 revenues were $839.6 million.

Above: Cerner Corporation employs about 3,200 people at its Kansas City headquarters.
Opposite page, top: Software designed by Transentric in St. Louis allows transportation companies to track shipments, transmit transactions, and more. Opposite page, bottom: Paper
charts are losing ground to Cerner Corporation's software at hospitals around the world.

Above: Missouri's information technology jobs tend to be concentrated in metropolitan areas, with higher numbers in Kansas City and in St. Louis, Boone, Wayne, Maries, Polk, Barry, and Lincoln Counties. Opposite page: More than 640,000 homes and businesses in Missouri have cable connections through St. Louis–based Charter Communications.

Transentric, a leader in Internet-based commerce software, makes sure no railcars are unaccounted for. Union Pacific in Nebraska founded the subsidiary in St. Louis in 1987 to focus on leveraging technological innovations in the railroad industry. Since then, Transentric has expanded its offerings to the trucking, agriculture, paper, beverage, and chemical industries, as well as to the public sector. Transentric's software allows companies to track and manage shipments, monitor supply chains, and communicate with trading partners. Companies can log on to the Internet for locations and estimated arrival times of their goods, helping to reduce labor, inventory, and equipment costs. Companies can also use Transentric's messaging service to electronically transmit transactions such as purchase orders and bills of lading. Transentric employs about 150 technology professionals to handle customers in the United States, Mexico, and Canada. Thousands of trading partners use Transentric's systems, which manage more than two million messages each week.

ALL WIRED UP

Instead of relocating to Dallas when their St. Louis cable company was bought during the early 1990s, executives Howard Wood, Barry Babcock, and Jerry Kent remained in Missouri to form Charter Communications in 1993. During the first four years, the company acquired 15 cable operations, maintained more than one million subscribers, and provided paging and high-speed cable Internet

services to some of its markets. In 1998, Microsoft cofounder Paul Allen assumed control of Charter Communications with a $4.5 billion investment. He led a flurry of acquisitions during the following years that ultimately established the company as a global leader in digital entertainment and communications, with networks designed to interconnect televisions, computers, the Internet, and other devices. Today, Charter Communications is the nation's third largest broadband communications company, wiring 6.3 million homes in 37 states. Revenues surpassed $4.8 billion in 2003.

HEADLINING THE SHOW-ME STATE

Pulitzer Inc. started because of a Hungarian immigrant who advocated truth and justice. In 1879, Joseph Pulitzer merged two daily newspapers in St. Louis to create the *St. Louis Post-Dispatch,* which is now the state's largest. Pulitzer's philosophy gained fame during the mid-1880s, when he bought the *New York World* and competed head-to-head with William Randolph Hearst's *New York Journal.* Their duel for readers erupted into a steady stream of sensational stories, creating the genre of yellow journalism. In 1903, Pulitzer established the prestigious Pulitzer prizes and donated $2 million to Columbia

University in New York for a journalism school. In 1912, Pulitzer's son, also named Joseph, assumed leadership of the St. Louis–based company. He acquired a St. Louis radio station in 1922 and a television station there in 1947. After his father's death, the third Joseph Pulitzer took over in 1955. He bought the *Daily Star* in Tucson in 1971. Pulitzer Inc. went public in 1986 and expanded in 1995, when it paid Scripps League Newspapers $214 million for 16 daily and 30 nondaily papers. Since the late 1990s, the company has continued to acquire publications and boost its Web site operations. Today, Pulitzer Inc. publishes 14 daily newspapers with related Internet operations and a

group of 37 weeklies in the St. Louis suburbs. Its flagship paper, the *St. Louis Post-Dispatch,* had a Sunday circulation of more than 468,000 in 2003. The Pulitzer family maintains a nearly 90 percent stake in its namesake company, which had sales of $422.7 million in 2003.

Another influential publication, this time for the sports world, also took shape in St. Louis. In 1886, Alfred H. Spink created "The Bible of Baseball" in St. Louis to please his barroom friends, who were avid sports fans. The first issue of *The Sporting News,* later universally referred to as baseball's bible, cost five cents and contained in-depth stories sprawled across an eight-page broadsheet. The publication achieved

Above: Long before becoming a media giant, Joseph Pulitzer attracted attention for his political views. Shown is a cartoon of Pulitzer as the "Leader of Liberal Republicanism" in the St. Louis *Puck,* published in 1872. Opposite page: For more than a century, readers have turned to the *St. Louis Post-Dispatch* for unbiased coverage of national and local issues. Shown are newspaper boys picking up the latest edition of the paper in 1910.

Above: In the 1940s, baseball was the main sport covered in *The Sporting News*. Shown, from left, are St. Louis Cardinals Marty Marion, Emil Verban, and Ray Sanders in 1944. Today, the St. Louis–based magazine covers all major sports. Opposite page, top: There are more than 30 daily newspapers in Missouri. Opposite page, bottom: Through its Cable in the Classroom program, Charter Communications provides free connections to more than 9,000 schools.

so much success that younger brother Charles Spink joined in the venture, eventually taking over. Charles Spink steered *The Sporting News* into an activist role, deploring umpire assaults and the peddling of alcohol in the stands, while laying the foundation for the World Series. Following Charles Spink's death in 1914, his son, J. G. Taylor Spink, took over. J. G. Taylor Spink broadened coverage to include football, basketball, and hockey, although baseball remained the primary focus. In 1943, he switched *The Sporting News* to a tabloid format to conserve paper in response to America's war efforts. In 1962, C. C. Johnson Spink succeeded his father and expanded content to all major sports, including golf, horse racing, soccer, the Olympics, tennis,

and other pastimes. In 1977, he sold the newspaper to media giant Times Mirror Company, which, in 1996, transformed the publication into a glossy magazine that gave football as much coverage as baseball. In 2000, the Times Mirror Company sold *The Sporting News* to Vulcan Ventures, an investment arm of Microsoft cofounder Paul Allen. Since then, *The Sporting News* has strengthened its sponsorship deals and on-line operations. With 1.9 million visitors per month, its Web site is a leading provider of fantasy sports games. The company owns and operates radio stations in New York, Los Angeles, Chicago, and Boston, and has more than 440 affiliates that together hook 13 million listeners weekly. The St. Louis–based company also publishes commemorative sports books and yearbooks, printing

approximately 50 titles annually. In early 2004, *The Sporting News* had a circulation of 715,000.

COMMUNITY MATTERS

Missouri's information technology, communications, and media companies connect communities through charity. Charter Communications' Cable in the Classroom program offers free cable and high-speed data connections to more than 9,000 schools. Each year, the *St. Louis Post-Dispatch* donates hundreds of thousands of dollars worth of free ad space for charities. Cerner Corporation's First Hand Foundation helps to fund uninsured families whose children have special medical needs. In 2003, the group received $915,000 in grants benefiting 3,100 children. Since the foundation began in 1995, it has funneled an estimated $2.6 million to nearly 6,000 young people.

MADE IN MISSOURI

Manufacturing

Local manufacturing companies wind their way into people's lives by producing coils and springs that make beds bounce, electric engines that drive objects big and small, computer chip coatings that keep machines humming, and more. Manufacturing is an important part of Missouri's economy, supplying more than 400,000 jobs and comprising 17 percent of the state's gross domestic product. Missouri's manufacturing abilities have secured its presence in the nation's living and working places.

A HALLMARK OF SUCCESS

Hallmark Cards embodies the rags-to-riches American spirit. Its founder, Joyce Clyde Hall, was a poor Nebraska teenager who dropped out of school in 1910 and boarded a Missouri-bound train with two shoeboxes of postcards—and even bigger dreams. Hall settled in Kansas City to sell cards to local stores. The following year, he and his brother, Rollie, opened a downtown gift store that featured postcards, stationery, and books. The Halls began offering greeting cards in 1912, and two years later, they created 20 engraved Christmas cards. A fire destroyed

Above and left: A diverse manufacturing base has helped Missouri to weather a nationwide slump in the sector. In fact, the state's manufacturing employment stabilized in 2003, bucking the national trend.

their inventory in 1915, leaving the brothers with a $17,000 debt, but they persevered by obtaining a loan, purchasing an engraving company, and creating their own cards. In 1917, an innovation was born when the brothers ran out of Christmas tissue and started selling decorated French envelope linings. From that, the gift wrapping industry emerged. In 1921, their brother, William Hall, joined the business, and two years later, the company incorporated as Hall Brothers. The word "Hallmark" debuted in 1925, and by 1928, it appeared on the back of every card.

Like many successful entrepreneurs, Joyce Hall trusted his intuition and embraced change. In the late 1920s, when his advisors cautioned him that advertising was a waste of money, Hall did it anyway,

eventually turning Hallmark into a household brand name. In 1951, despite warnings, Hall launched a series of television specials that became known as the *Hallmark Hall of Fame.* Since then, the specials have won nearly 80 Emmy awards. Hall's foresight extended

into real estate as well—in the late 1960s, he spearheaded the development of Crown Center, an entertainment complex in Kansas City. The 85-acre center, credited with revitalizing downtown, encompasses restaurants, shops, a residential community, hotels, and office

buildings, including Hallmark Cards' international headquarters.

After Hall's death in 1982, his son, and later, his grandson, continued to run the company. Hallmark Cards expanded its customer base by offering niche cards for African-Americans, Jews, Christians, women, and Spanish-speakers. It also introduced an overnight flower delivery service and acquired more businesses, including the maker of Crayola Crayons and a portrait studio chain. Today, the company's cards can be found in more than 42,000 retail stores nationwide. Hallmark Cards also distributes goods to more than 100 countries and employs more than 19,000 people worldwide. The company had consolidated net revenues of $4.3 billion in 2003.

CONVENIENCE, COMFORT, AND CARE

Missouri's highest ranking Fortune 500 company, Emerson, started small in 1890, after two Scottish brothers, Charles and Alexander Meston, convinced John Wesley Emerson to invest in their idea for a business focused on electric motors. Two years later, the St. Louis company sold the nation's first electric fans, establishing an esteemed reputation among consumers. Eventually the company applied electric motors to household and commercial items such as sewing machines, power tools, dental drills, and player pianos. During World War II, Emerson was the largest producer of aircraft gun

Above: Once a painstaking process, greeting card production was revolutionized by the computer. Shown is an artist working on Christmas cards in 1942. Opposite page, top: Joyce Hall, founder of Hallmark Cards in Kansas City, understood the importance of marketing. In 1928, Hallmark Cards was the first greeting card company to advertise nationally. Opposite page, bottom: Hallmark Cards employs about 5,000 people in its Kansas City headquarters.

Above: St. Louis–based Emerson manufactures process field devices and automation products that are used in chemical plants. Opposite page, top: Emerson's power supply products can keep hospitals running during power outages. Opposite page, bottom: By the 1890s, Emerson had a second shop in St. Louis.

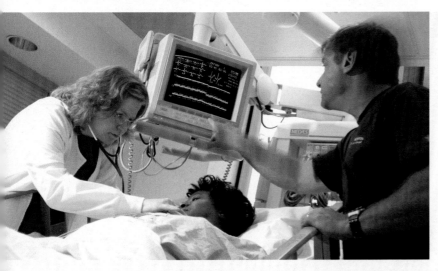

turrets in the world. After the war, the company focused on expansion. By 1954, Emerson had 4,000 employees and two plants, and by 1973, it had 31,000 workers and 82 facilities. Since then, Emerson has grown globally to more than 120,000 employees in more than 60 divisions and 320 manufacturing operations. Three manufacturing facilities are in Missouri. From convenience in air-conditioning, appliances, and storage systems to power supplies that protect phone and computer networks, its products touch consumers and businesses worldwide. Emerson's sales reached $14 billion in fiscal 2003.

Leggett & Platt, another Missouri Fortune 500 company, changed the way people sleep. During the 1800s, most people slept on mattresses made of feathers, cotton, or horsehair. That began to change in 1883, when J. P. Leggett, an inventor from Carthage, and his businessman brother-in-law, C. B. Platt, started selling spiral steel coil bedsprings. In 1885, the L&P bedspring was patented, and in 1901, the business incorporated. By the 1930s, Leggett & Platt produced different types of springs such as those used in upholstered furniture. Throughout the decades, the company continued to build its operation, adding plants and acquiring businesses that allowed it to bounce into other markets. Still based in Carthage, Leggett & Platt makes springs and spring units; headboards; commercial store displays and shelves; components for outdoor lighting fixtures and gas barbecue grills; industrial materials; quilting machinery; and more. The company has 31,000 employees and 300

Above: Spring mattresses, made popular by Carthage-based Leggett & Platt, inspired other companies to make similar products. Shown is one such company in 1933. Opposite page, top: Produced by Faultless/Bon Ami Company in Kansas City, Bon Ami is the country's third best-selling powdered cleanser. Shown are products from 1886 to 1978. Opposite page, bottom: Bon Ami's familiar slogan, "Hasn't Scratched Yet," appeared as early as the 1880s.

The Owl and the Pussy Cat. During the 1960s, Faultless Starch developed fabric finish, hot iron cleaner, spray prewash, and aerosol starch, catapulting the aerosol starch category into one of the fastest growing segments in U.S. supermarkets. In 1974, the business became Faultless Starch/Bon Ami Company after it acquired Bon Ami cleaning products. The Bon Ami trademark represents about a five percent share in the nation's cleanser business, distinguishing it as the third best-selling powdered cleanser. The company also sells more than 75 starches and chemicals to commercial dry cleaners and laundries. Faultless Starch/Bon Ami Company's headquarters, laboratory, and distribution center are in

facilities in 18 countries; 19 of its manufacturing plants are in Missouri. In 2003, Leggett & Platt had revenues of $4.3 billion.

Faultless/Bon Ami Company's products are used in American homes and businesses as well. The company traces its heritage to 1886, when Major Thomas G. Beaham moved from Ohio to Kansas City and purchased the formula for Faultless Starch. In 1891, he named

his company after the dry white product, which had quickly gained popularity among American housewives because it required no boiling, treated skin irritations, and soothed baby bottoms. During the 1890s, a Faultless salesman named John Nesbitt bolstered the company's profile by distributing wagonloads of starch boxes wrapped with Faultless Starch books, whose titles included *Mother Goose Rhymes* and

Kansas City; manufacturing facilities are in Kansas City and Humansville. The Beaham family still owns and operates the business.

PRODUCTS TAKING SHAPE

At Spartech Corporation, plastic reigns. The company takes plastic resins and makes them into calendered film, finished molded products, plastic alloys, sheet, and rollstock. Lawrence Powers, a former attorney, started the company in 1960. At the time, the business had nonplastic divisions such as copper tubing and electronics, but by the 1980s, Spartech Corporation turned to plastics, the dominant focus ever since. Today, the company is North America's largest producer of sheet and rollstock and a leading maker of polymeric compounds and engineered thermoplastics materials. Spartech Corporation's 7,000-plus clients include packaging companies and businesses that make electronics, toys, auto parts, and building materials. It boasts 43 facilities in North America and Europe. In Missouri, the company has headquarters in Clayton, a St. Louis suburb, and two facilities in Cape Girardeau. Each year, the company processes more than 1.2 billion pounds of molded and profile products, color and specialty compounds, custom sheet and rollstock, and plastic alloys. In fiscal 2003, Spartech Corporation posted $956.2 million in sales, a six percent increase over the previous year.

Like Spartech Corporation, Brewer Science specializes in chemical compound manufacturing. Terry and Paula Brewer founded the business in 1981 to provide the microelectronics industry with organic chemical technology designed to increase efficiency and productivity. The company, which started with three employees and an office in Rolla, introduced the first organic antireflective coating for computer chip makers in 1982. Four years later, Brewer Science became a provider of coaters for optoelectronic products. Today, it is a leading developer and supplier of thin-film polymer coatings used in the microelectronic, optoelectronic, and sensor industries, as well as wafer processing equipment. The firm employs more than 300 people worldwide and has more than 1,000 clients. A facility in Rolla houses Brewer Science's headquarters, product development, and manufacturing plants.

NURTURING THE COMMUNITY

Manufacturers in Missouri offer more than products. Since 1997, Hallmark Cards has donated cards with detachable immunization schedules to state governments. Parents of approximately three million newborns receive the reminders each year. The company also encourages its employees to volunteer by contributing $200 to nonprofits where workers have spent time. Emerson has given more than $206 million to community groups and centers nationwide since 1981. It contributed to the 92,000-square-foot Emerson Center at the Missouri Historical Society in St. Louis, which opened in 2000. In 2003, Emerson donated $20 million to groups nationwide focused on education, youth, civics, health, human services, art, and culture. Leggett & Platt was a majority sponsor of a $7.5 million, 80,000-square-foot athletic center at Missouri Southern State University in Joplin that opened in 1999.

This page, top: Plastics and rubber products are among Missouri's top exports. This page, bottom: Brewer Science in Rolla, a manufacturer of thin-film polymer coatings, has more than 45 patents to its credit. Opposite page: Missouri's plastics manufacturers produce everything from film, sheets, and bags to pipes and bottles.

GETTING DOWN TO BUSINESS

Professional and Business-to-Business Services

Whether championing the nation's businesswomen or leading one of the world's largest communications agencies, people in Missouri work hard. They also work together. It is an ethos that permeates the state, providing a breeding ground for companies specializing in professional and business-to-business services. Success for one professional, or one business, translates into success for Missouri.

PROFESSIONALISM AT ITS BEST
Despite its status as the oldest law firm west of the Mississippi River, Lathrop & Gage considers itself young. Founded in Kansas City in 1873, the firm still represents its first client, Burlington Northern Santa Fe Railroad, then known as Atchison, Topeka & Santa Fe Railroad Co. The company melds old with new by being quick to adapt to new

technology. Lathrop & Gage was one of the nation's first firms to offer a wireless Web site that allows clients to access the computer page via cell phone. The firm also saw the dot-com bust as an opportunity to hire tech industry legal eagles to bolster its intellectual property department—a department that grew from one attorney to 30 during a five-year period. The firm's charge-ahead

Above and left: People seeking legal assistance can choose from approximately 20,000 lawyers who practice in Missouri. Local law firms specialize in everything from business and consumer law to family and probate law.

approach reflects the spirit of its founders, prominent attorneys Gardiner Lathrop and John B. (Jack) Gage. In 2003, Lathrop & Gage had more than 230 attorneys, 25 practice areas, and seven offices in the Midwest and Washington, D.C.

Another professional services firm started in St. Louis, this time in 1973, when a group of engineers established a consulting service now known as EDM. The firm quickly gained a reputation for possessing

expertise in building structures for family-entertainment attractions. In 1986, EDM provided structural engineering for the redevelopment of Union Station in St. Louis. During the 1990s, EDM's structural engineers designed projects for the St. Louis Rams domed stadium, casinos at the St. Charles Riverfront Station, and cool pools for animals at Sea World Orlando. EDM also offers service in industries ranging from retail and recreation to health

care and hospitality. In 2000, it opened a branch office in Fairview Heights, Illinois. Approximately 34 architects, engineers, and planners work for the company.

Missouri's commitment to hard work paved the way for one of the nation's most successful professional women's associations. In the 1940s, the term businesswoman was an anomaly. Women who had entered the workforce during World War II to fill in while men fought overseas

Above: The redevelopment of Union Station in St. Louis was the country's largest adaptive reuse project at the time. St. Louis—based EDM provided structural engineering for the project. Opposite page, top and bottom: About 50,000 women belong to the American Business Women's Association in Kansas City, which was inspired by the women who went to work during World War II.

were expected to leave their jobs once soldiers returned. Hilary A. Bufton Jr., a Kansas City businessman, thought that would be a loss to the American economy—and to women who enjoyed working outside of the home.

So Bufton and three Kansas City career women formed the American Business Women's Association in 1949 to provide women with networking opportunities and professional development. In the

mid-1960s, Bufton's wife, Ruth, took over the organization when he was struck with a serious illness. The American Business Women's Association gained momentum, and in 1983, President Ronald Reagan proclaimed September 22nd American Business Women's Day to celebrate the accomplishments of the group as well as millions of working women. Today, Hilary and Ruth Bufton's daughter, Carolyn Bufton Elman, serves as executive director, staying true to the group's founding focus while adapting to a changing workforce. The association studies business trends and forges alliances, including ones with the Ewing Marion Kauffman Foundation and Franklin Covey, which, respectively, emphasize entrepreneurial success and time-management strategies. In 2003, the organization began offering

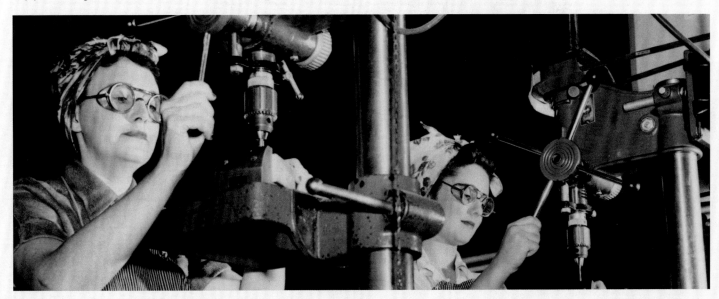

master's degree classes in business taught by instructors at the University of Kansas School of Business and its KU Center for Management Education. The American Business Women's Association maintains its national headquarters in Kansas City and has 50,000 members.

BUSINESSES
HELPING BUSINESSES

Inside a St. Louis five-and-dime in 1946, Al Fleishman and Bob Hillard founded what would become one of the world's leading communications agencies. During the first few decades, Fleishman-Hillard focused on regional clients. That changed in 1966, when the firm hired John Graham, a young executive determined to expand the company's presence to locations far

and wide. Since Graham became president and chief executive officer in 1974, Fleishman-Hillard has swelled to more than 80 offices throughout North America, Latin America, Asia, Europe, Australia, and South Africa. The agency's services range from public relations, marketing, and

public affairs to interactive design. During the past two decades, the firm has achieved a 25 percent compound growth rate while working for clients such as Hallmark Cards, Wal-Mart, Emerson, and Anheuser-Busch. In 1997, Fleishman-Hillard became part of New York City–based Omnicom Group, one of the world's leading advertising and marketing communications companies. Fleishman-Hillard's headquarters remain in St. Louis.

One of Missouri's first full-service environmental, health, and safety consulting companies began in Kansas City. In 1983, Duncan Heydon and Skuli Gudmundsson founded OCCU-TEC, recognizing that businesses were scurrying to comply with—and often confused about—a growing number of environmental laws and regulations. OCCU-TEC helps businesses to address immediate safety concerns

Above: Businesses that must comply with complicated environmental laws turn to consulting companies to guide them through the process. Opposite page, top and bottom: Communications agencies bolster their clients' profiles through business-to-consumer marketing, interactive communications, and more.

Above: Environmental consulting firms can devise plans for handling hazardous materials. Opposite page, top: Small businesses looking to expand their operations often seek advice from consulting companies. Opposite page, bottom: Scholarships funded by Missouri's professional and business-to-business companies are offering students unique opportunities.

and reduce the potential for liability. The company custom-designs plans in a range of categories, including remediation and asbestos and lead assessments, along with management of air quality, underground storage tanks, water resources, and hazardous materials. In 2002, OCCU-TEC teamed with Eastern Michigan University to provide on-line health and safety training courses as a cost-effective approach to increasing workplace safety. In 2003, the company employed 17 people who service clients nationwide, in both the public and private sector.

A strong business ethic also inspired Hochschild, Bloom & Company to set up shop in Chesterfield, a St. Louis suburb. On New Year's Day, 1952, Peter Hochschild and Melvin Bloom forged a company composed mostly of certi-fied public accountants. Although Hochschild, Bloom & Company helps clients with accounting and tax issues, the company's mission has

grown during the last half-century. The firm's accountants, consultants, and advisors offer a range of services, including overall business improve-ment with an emphasis in areas such as small business development, manu-facturing operations, computer con-sulting, and more. While larger firms often present full-service menus, it is uncommon for a company the size of Hochschild, Bloom & Company, which has 42 employees. The firm has

approximately 1,700 clients a year and has an additional office in Washington, Missouri.

MENTORING THE FUTURE

Future businesspeople are benefit-ting from Missouri's professional and business-to-business companies. Since 1953, the American Business Women's Association has granted approximately 13,400 scholarships totaling more than $13 million through its Stephen Bufton Memorial Educational Fund. Each year, Fleishman-Hillard recruits and trains college students through its Multicultural Communications Scholarships program, which awards $2,500 to $5,000 toward tuition assistance. Students also spend their summers gaining experience as paid interns at Fleishman-Hillard offices.

DESTINATION MISSOURI
Tourism, Hospitality, and Retail

They come for Missouri's trees and theaters. Bluffs and bass shops. Hillsides and hotels. With natural and man-made attractions, the state beckons. In 2003, approximately 34.7 million people visited the state, spending $7.7 billion.

THAT'S ENTERTAINMENT

Nestled in Missouri's Ozark Mountains, Branson's tourist attractions draw millions of visitors. The vacation destination has become one of the nation's entertainment hubs, boasting more than 40 theaters for musical acts, with 60,000 theater seats and more than 70 live theater shows. It has lakes, family entertainment centers, championship golf courses, theme parks, restaurants, and lodging. It has come a long way since 1903, when the town was founded with visions of becoming a major exporter of manufactured products, lumber, and logs. By the time Branson incorporated in 1912, the city realized it could become a resort. In the years that followed, entrepreneurs targeted the waterfront area, starting candy and ice cream factories and a soft drink bottling plant. Hobart McQuarter, a local businessman, constructed Sammy Lane Resort, the town's first vacation resort.

Above: The Hollywood Wax Museum in Branson has memorialized John Wayne, Elvis Presley, Marilyn Monroe, and Charlie Chaplin in a Mount Rushmore—style tribute. Left: Retail sales totaled $29.6 billion in Missouri in 2002.

By the 1930s, leisure activities, including boat races on Lake Taneycomo, spurred Branson's reputation as a thrifty recreation destination. In 1959, The Baldknobbers Hillbilly Jamboree Show opened, the city's first musical performance. Two years later, workers finished Table Rock Dam, protecting the waterfront from flooding and providing visitors with a new, big lake. Tourism flourished during the 1960s and 1970s as highways and bridges were built in and around Branson. With the roads sprouted more motels, merchants, eateries, and entertainment venues. The town's development boomed Branson's music scene, one that has grown in size and status during the past three decades. Today, tourism is a $1.7 billion-a-year industry in Branson.

SILVER DOLLAR GOLD

Beginning in 1946, Hugo and Mary Herschend, wildflower enthusiasts from Wilmette, Illinois, traveled each year to Missouri's Ozark hillsides to admire native blossoms. The couple also fell in love with Marvel Cave in Branson. Seeking retirement income, Hugo leased the cave in 1950 and bought 640 acres surrounding the landmark shortly after. He turned his beloved find into a profitable tourist business. After acquiring the cave, Hugo created the first cable car system in a North American cave. By the summer of 1952, the Herschends had

Above: Each year, more than 7.2 million people visit Branson. Shown is busy 76 Country Boulevard. Opposite page, top: Silver Dollar City in Branson captures the spirit of a 19th-century American mining town. Opposite page, bottom: A sea lion sunbathes at the St. Louis Zoo, where more than 9,200 animals live.

hosted 8,000 visitors to their Ozark property. After Hugo's death in 1955, his wife, Mary, and their eldest son, Jack, continued his dream. With $18,000 from a bank, the Herschends and their employees began building a cable railway system in 1957 that would explore the cave's depths. The train opened to the public the following year. The family, including younger son Peter, pursued Hugo's original vision of reconstructing their property into a 19th-century mining town with a general store, ice cream parlor, blacksmith, doll shop, and picture-window church. It opened in 1960, and they named it Silver Dollar City because employees gave visitors admission change in silver dollars. Each year, more than two million people attend the 47-acre theme park, which offers 17 rides and attractions, 60 shops and restaurants, 50 shows a day, and annual festivals. In early 2003, Silver Dollar City Inc. changed

its name to Herschend Family Entertainment Corporation and opened a $40 million theme park in Branson called Celebration City. The company, based in Branson, owns or operates 17 properties in seven states.

Animal Houses

The St. Louis Zoo exists because residents craved a world-class zoo. The push began in 1904, when animal exhibits at the World's Fair in Forest

Park piqued interest in a zoological park. When the exposition ended that year, St. Louis residents paid $3,500 for the Smithsonian Institution's walk-through birdcage. In 1910, the Zoological Society of St. Louis formed to establish a zoo. Six years later, St. Louis citizens voted to tax themselves for building a zoo on 77 acres in Forest Park. The St. Louis Zoo is believed to be the world's first zoo supported by a community passing a mill tax. Construction immediately followed. In 1972, St. Louis city and county voters passed a Zoo/Museum District Tax and approved raising it 11 years later. The money went toward repairs, renovations, and new exhibits. In 1993, the zoo expanded by 355 acres with the donation of a nearby farm for breeding endangered species. Nearly 100 years after the St. Louis Zoo's founding, approximately three

Above: The St. Louis Zoo has captivated visitors with unique exhibits for nearly a century. In 2003, the zoo opened North America's first walk-through subantarctic penguin habitat. Opposite page, top: Free evening beverages is one of the signature services offered by St. Louis–based Drury Inns. Opposite page, bottom: There are more than 30 Drury Inns properties in Missouri.

million animal enthusiasts visit the zoo each year, ranking it fifth nationally in annual attendance.

HOMES AWAY FROM HOME

Born in Fairview in 1919, James Quentin Hammons learned about hard work on his family's struggling dairy farm. Nicknamed John Q., he worked in wheat fields to pay for college. As a young adult, he risked—and sometimes lost— thousands of dollars on business ventures. It was not until 1958, when Hammons, with a partner, found his calling in hotel development. He bought Holiday Inn franchises and by the late 1960s, had developed more than three dozen hotels. In 1973, Hammons was running roughly 35 hotels. He focused on high-end, full-service accommo-

dations and realized the value of convention center hotels early on. He also foresaw the growth of towns and cities, building hotels near highways. In 1994, John Q. Hammons Hotels, based in Springfield, went public, providing Hammons with money to develop more hotels. Open to innovation

and fearless of risks, Hammons turned his company into one of the nation's top independent hotel developers. Today, the business owns and operates more than 50 hotels. It is also an industry leader in building and managing the nation's hotel meeting and convention spaces. In 2003, sales reached more than $431.2 million.

Lambert Drury, another successful Missouri hotelier, started his career in a different field as well. In the 1940s, he owned a plastering business in the Missouri Bootheel with his sons. In 1973, however, the Drurys decided to try a new venture: running a limited-service hotel. The family opened the first Drury Inn in Sikeston, with a rate of $10.88 a night. The hotel presented customers with clean and pleasant accommodations, while providing rooms at rates approximately 25 percent below those of its full-service competitors. In 1986, Drury Inns marked a first in its business niche by offering guests quick and free breakfasts. In 1998, the lodging chain unveiled free evening beverages and snacks. In three decades, the St. Louis–based hotel chain has grown from one inn to more than 100 hotels in 17 states.

SHOPPING SENSATIONS

May Department Stores Company, the nation's second largest operator of upscale department stores, started in 1877, when David May opened a store in the mining town of Leadville, Colorado. By 1905, May and his business partners had bought clothing and department stores in St. Louis and Cleveland. Needing a place to base the company, May chose St. Louis, a mid-American city

basking in the success of the 1904 World's Fair. The May Department Stores Company incorporated in 1910, with earnings reaching $1 million. In 1911, May's business landed on the New York Stock Exchange. That year, May also

purchased the William Barr Dry Goods Company in St. Louis and merged it with The Famous Clothing Store he bought in 1892. Together, they formed Famous-Barr, one of the company's six department store divisions. In 2003, the May

FAMOUS-BARR
COMPANY
SAINT LOUIS • MISSOURI

Above: Famous-Barr is one of six department store divisions owned by May Department Stores Company in St. Louis. Shown is a catalog from the 1920s. Opposite page, top and bottom: Famous-Barr has occupied part of the Railway Exchange Building in St. Louis since the building was completed in 1914. Top is a postcard rendering of the building when it first opened; bottom is the building in the 1960s.

Above: Outdoor World in Springfield, Bass Pro Shop's flagship store and headquarters, features a 40,000-square-foot boat showroom. Opposite page, top: Each day, visitors can watch divers feed fish at Outdoor World. Opposite page, bottom: Fishing enthusiasts around the country head to Bass Pro Shops for bait, rods, tackle, and other equipment.

attraction, luring more than four million visitors a year. The company operates 21 shops in 14 states. In 2003, Bass Pro Shops was the world's largest sports cataloger, mailing more than 30 million catalogs a year.

MISSOURI BENEVOLENCE

Missouri's retailers recognize the value of charity. Since 2000, Bass Pro Shops has donated more than $30 million to groups such as the International Game Fish Association, the National Fish and Wildlife Foundation, and the Wonders of Wildlife National Museum. May Department Stores Company contributed $16 million to more than 2,000 nonprofits nationwide in 2002. Additionally, May employees gave $5.7 million to the United Way and other charities.

Department Stores Company operated 445 department stores using 11 trade names in 37 states and the District of Columbia. Some of its regional stores include Famous-Barr, Robinsons-May, David's Bridal, Filene's, Foley's, and Kaufmann's. The company's 2003 sales totaled more than $13.4 billion.

Bass Pro Shops, the world's largest supplier of outdoor gear, started an industry in 1972. Before then, no large-scale, streamlined source existed for anglers to buy specialized gear needed for the burgeoning sport of tournament fishing. Johnny Morris recognized that need, opening the first Bass Pro Shops in Springfield. In 1974, the merchant mailed its first catalog. Three years later, Bass Pro Shops launched packages with Tracker Boats, which became the world's top seller of fishing boats. The company's success

led to the 1984 opening of Outdoor World, its flagship store and headquarters in Springfield. Four years later, the company unveiled Big Cedar Lodge, a lakeside resort in Missouri's Ozark Mountains. Bass Pro Shops continued to grow during the 1990s. Today, its 300,000-square-foot flagship store is a tourist

MOVING FORWARD
Transportation, Utilities, and Energy

Missouri has power. At any given moment, its utilities and energy companies fuel homes and businesses around the state and the world. Missouri also generates commerce. Boats chug down its rivers. Planes fly above its land. Trains travel through its towns. Vehicles zip along its roads. All of which ensures that the state is driving toward a bright future.

WATERWAYS AND AIRWAYS

From the Mississippi River, St. Louis emerged. The young and growing city relied on the muddy waterway for sustenance. Businesses bustled along the banks. River trading in agricultural products and furs provided an economic foundation. Situated near the confluence of the Mississippi, Missouri, and Illinois Rivers, St. Louis offered powerful opportunities for river commerce, allowing the industry—and the city—to mature. Today, the city remains indebted to its riverfront. The Port of Metropolitan St. Louis stretches 80 miles along the Mississippi River, from Madison County, Illinois, to Jefferson County, Missouri. Moored barges and industrial terminals line the waterway. Stacks of fertilizer, steel, lumber, coal,

Above: Missouri's major airports move people in Missouri and beyond. In 2003, 29.6 million people traveled through Lambert–St. Louis International Airport and Kansas City International Airport, combined. **Left.** In 2002, 136 utilities companies provided energy to Missourians.

Above: In 1959, Trans World Airlines chose Lambert–St. Louis International Airport to inaugurate its Boeing 707 service. Shown is the airport in the 1950s. Opposite page, top: Missouri's transportation industry employed more than 196,800 people in 2002. Opposite page, bottom: There are about 130 public-use airports in the state.

and other commodities await handling. It is the nation's third largest inland port by cargo volume, overseeing nearly 35 million tons of freight each year.

Missouri's airways also hum. In 2003, 20.4 million passengers traveled through Lambert–St. Louis International Airport, the 18th busiest in North America. The airport, however, began as a small balloon-launch field. Major Albert Lambert envisioned it as a hub for the growing aviation industry and in 1920, converted a 170-acre hay field into an airfield. Seven years later, Lambert offered to sell Lambert Field to the city of St. Louis for $68,352, the amount he paid for it. He also owned 380 surrounding acres, which the city received through a $2 million bond issue. In 1928,

Lambert–St. Louis Municipal Airport became the nation's first city-owned airport. A decade later, 40,000 passengers were arriving and departing from the airport annually. During World War II, air travel slowed, but the area's aviation industry took off with the manufacture of more than 3,000 military

planes. In 1956, the new domed design for Lambert's main terminal became a prototype for modern airports, inspiring plans for John F. Kennedy Airport in New York City and Charles de Gaulle Airport in Paris. Lambert continued to prosper as air travel gained popularity. In 1959, Trans World Airlines inaugurated Boeing 707 service at Lambert. About this time, McDonnell Douglas Aircraft Corporation also used the airport for building the Mercury series spacecraft. During the mid-1970s, Lambert extended its facilities, increasing its gate and operational capacities. In 2003, Lambert encompassed 2,000 acres, with an airfield composed of five runways serving nine major airlines, 10 commuter services, and two charter companies. The airport is currently undergoing a $1.1 billion expansion, with projected

completion in 2006. The plan
includes building a two-mile-long
runway and buying more than
1,500 acres.

GROUNDED BUSINESSES

Enterprise Rent-A-Car began with a
hunch. In 1957, Jack Taylor figured
there must be an easier way to earn a
living than selling cars for a Cadillac
dealership in St. Louis. Years of lis-
tening to clients' needs encouraged
Taylor to start a leasing business in

the dealership's body shop. Again,
Taylor heeded the words of his customers, who asked to rent cars while
theirs were being fixed. Taylor added
a daily rental component to his company during the 1960s. He and his
business team decided not to compete
with firms dominating the market
such as Avis and Hertz. Instead, they
focused on the replacement market,
offering good rates to insurance
adjusters looking for temporary transportation for policyholders. In 1969,

Taylor expanded beyond Missouri and
into Georgia, opening the first branch
office in Atlanta. The early 1970s provided more opportunities for growth,
as Taylor established operations in
Texas and Florida. Skyrocketing oil
prices, however, compelled the company to test other markets, including
buying a supplier of beverages and
packaged foods to prison commis-
saries. In 1976, Taylor introduced
Enterprise Fleet Services, which targeted large companies needing to buy
or lease more than 50 vehicles.
During the 1980s, the firm continued
to acquire car businesses and suppliers
of products ranging from tea for hotel
guests to hygiene products for pris-
oners. By this time, Taylor's son,
Andrew, or "Andy," served as the
company's second president. With his
father, Andy Taylor drove Enterprise

Rent-A-Car's success, increasing its brand recognition with national television ads. He also shifted focus to discretionary rentals, for instance to families with out-of-town visitors. In 1996, with more than 500,000 vehicles, the company climbed to the top as the largest car rental company in North America. During this time, additional offices opened in Europe. In 1999, it spun nonautomotive businesses into the Centric Group and expanded airport operations to target occasional travelers. Enterprise Rent-A-Car now runs businesses in or near the country's top 100 airports, offering lower rates than those of most of the industry giants. In 2001, Andy Taylor became the company's chairman and chief executive officer, and the first family outsider, Donald Ross, assumed the presidency. Presently, the St. Louis–based firm has more than 5,000 branches worldwide. In fiscal 2003, sales reached $6.9 billion.

The nation's largest private trucking group owner also calls Missouri home. UniGroup formed in 1987 when moving company executives combined United Van Lines and Mayflower Transit, two of the leading operations in transporting household goods. UniGroup also oversees related subsidiaries that offer movers insurance, sell and lease vehicles and packaging supplies, and more. Based in Fenton, the company coordinates centralized support for all of its worldwide operations, including purchasing, facilities management,

Above: United Van Lines, owned by UniGroup in Fenton, boasts an on-time delivery rate of more than 99 percent. Shown is a United Van Lines truck in the early 1950s. Opposite page, top: Enterprise Rent-A-Car's fleet has grown from 17 cars in 1963 to more than 559,000 in 2003. The St. Louis–based firm is the largest car rental company in North America. Opposite page, bottom: Missouri's trucking companies make moving easier.

and mail and supply centers. Approximately 250 company managers for UniGroup companies and active agents of United Van Lines and Mayflower Transit own the firm. UniGroup transports household and office goods in more than 100 countries.

Utilitarian Forces

Aquila is all about energy. It has been the company's focus since 1917, when its founder, Lemuel Green, bought a utility in Pleasant Hill. Throughout the decades, the Kansas City–based company has changed names, acquired businesses, and closed operations. Its ability to adapt in a competitive industry speaks for its success. Formerly UtiliCorp United, Aquila owns electricity and gas distribution networks serving an estimated 1.3 million customers in seven states. The company's subsidiaries deliver energy to Canada and the United Kingdom. In 2003, Aquila's total assets reached $8.4 billion.

The Laclede Group, another major utility in Missouri, warms the St. Louis region, as it has done since its founding in 1857. Back then, the company supplied light to northern parts of St. Louis. It also produced and vended gas, gas lights, and gas fixtures. Today, the company's main subsidiary, Laclede Gas Company, ranks as the state's largest natural gas distributor, serving 630,000 customers in eastern Missouri. The St. Louis utility also transports and stores liquid propane and runs underground natural gas storage fields. The company's other operations include wholesale gas marketing and real estate development. The Laclede Group's revenues reached more than $1 billion in fiscal 2003.

World Powerhouse

Peabody Energy fuels power plants. Headquartered in St. Louis, the business is among the world's largest coal companies, providing energy and services to more than 270 generating and industrial-client locations in 33 states and 11 countries. Peabody Energy's achievement stems from its focus on generating electricity from coal, which costs less than other fossil fuels. Coal is also cleaner, with emissions from coal plants decreasing by one-third

Above: Additional natural gas is often pumped into underground storage tanks in preparation for the cold winter months. Opposite page, top: Easy to transport, propane gas can be used in places natural gas pipelines do not reach. Opposite page, bottom: Laclede Gas Company, a subsidiary of St. Louis–based Laclede Group, supplies natural gas to customers in nine eastern Missouri counties.

Above: The vast majority of electricity in Missouri is generated by coal, with nuclear generation coming in at a distant second. Opposite page, top: Twelve utilities companies operate large fossil-fueled power plants in the state. Opposite page, bottom: Peabody Energy in St. Louis supplied 203 million tons of coal to clients around the world in 2003.

during the past three decades while coal-based electricity generation nearly tripled. Each year, Peabody Energy produces more than 190 million tons of coal and preserves more than nine billion tons in reserves. Nationwide, the company operates approximately 33 mines and processing facilities, including coal-bed methane production, coal trading, and the development of coal-based generating plants. It provides fuel for more than 9 percent of power in the United States and more than 2 percent in the world. In 2003, the company sold 203 million tons with revenues of $2.8 billion. Peabody Energy's growth reflects the conviction of Francis S. Peabody, who believed in the benefits of coal and founded the company in 1883.

CHARITABLE COMMODITIES

The state's energy and transportation companies energize communities. Peabody Energy strives to keep the environment healthy by overseeing the planting of nearly one million trees a year, as well as projects that reintroduce wildlife and fish onto mined lands. Since its founding in 1957, Enterprise Rent-A-Car, its foundation, and the Taylor family have endowed nearly $150 million to charitable causes. Some recent contributions

include $40 million to the renowned Saint Louis Symphony Orchestra, $30 million to the Missouri Botanical Garden for global plant research, and $25 million in scholarships for African-American and low-income students. Enterprise Rent-A-Car also gave $10 million to the Naval Aviation Museum Foundation in Pensacola, Florida; $2 million to the National Urban League; and $1 million to victims of the September 11, 2001, terrorist attacks.

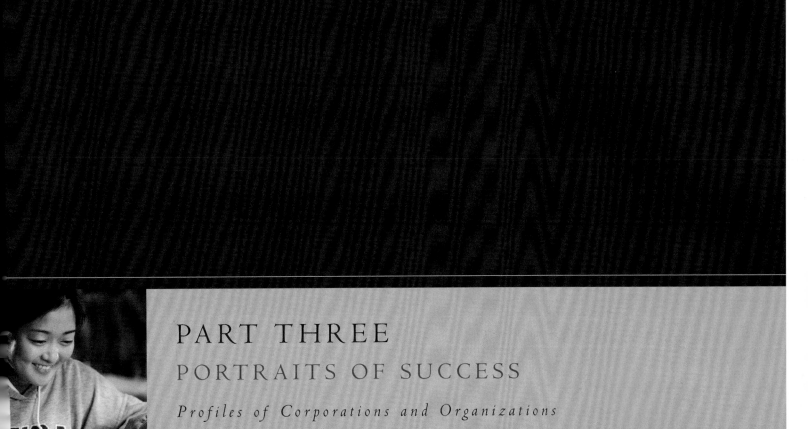

PART THREE

PORTRAITS OF SUCCESS

Profiles of Corporations and Organizations

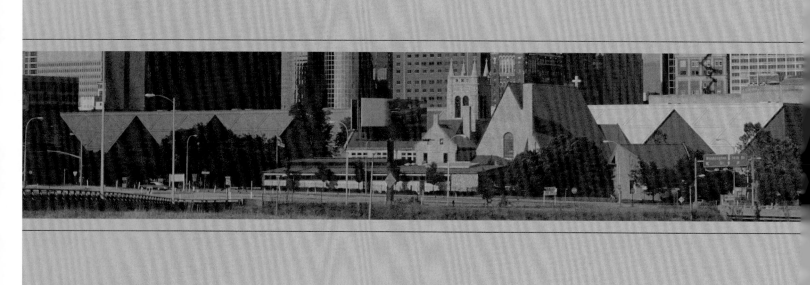

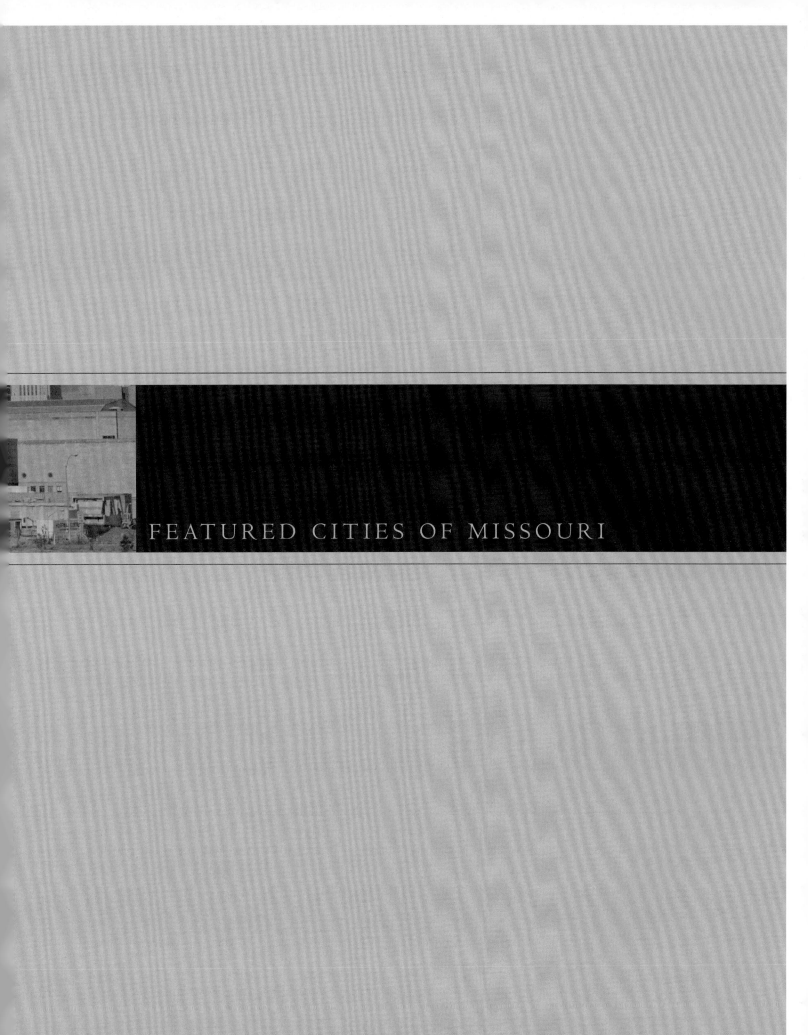

FEATURED CITIES OF MISSOURI

CITY OF KANSAS CITY, MISSOURI

As the city sweeps top national rankings in categories from job growth to livability, the Economic Development Corporation of Kansas City, Missouri, continues in its tireless role as facilitator to the business community in this thriving City of Fountains.

This historic and graceful City of Fountains is also a city of numerous works of public art. *The Scout,* by Cyrus E. Dallin, watches over downtown Kansas City—ranked as one of the top 10 "most livable places of the decade" (by Partners for Livable Communities) and as one of the top 10 U.S. cities for attracting new business (by *Expansion Management* magazine).

Kansas City, Missouri, is an ideal location for business. At the center of the nation, the city is a natural transportation hub and a logical site for corporate headquarters. It is one of the country's largest rail hubs and one of the five largest trucking centers. Kansas City International Airport, on 10,000 acres, is one of the largest airfields in the country and moves the fourth largest amount of cargo on the NAFTA air corridor—yet the airport is known for being convenient, people friendly, and uncongested. Kansas City ranks in the top 10

U.S. cities for attracting new business, according to *Expansion Management* magazine, and in the top 10 as well for job growth. It is also renowned as one of the best places to do business electronically, rating fifth in the nation for percentage of broadband Internet use.

The city works for people as well as business. Recognized as a great place to live, work, and play, downtown Kansas City made the top 10 list of "most livable places of the decade," published in 2004 by Partners for Livable Communities.

The list of pluses goes on—thanks in no small part to the Economic Development Corporation of Kansas City, Missouri (EDC). The private, nonprofit organization has worked since 1987 to promote economic development, facilitate redevelopment, encourage investment, and otherwise help companies that are doing business in the city.

The group's full-time staff of development officers takes seriously its mission to maintain and increase the number of private sector jobs. Through a variety of programs and services, the staff actively assists firms to start up and grow in Kansas City, and to relocate to Kansas City. The organization can provide information and counseling on industry issues, financing, and incentives; find qualified job applicants and employee training or retraining programs; help with site selection and other development needs; advocate in governmental matters at city, region, and state levels; and assist in the permitting and regulatory process. In addition, the nonprofit EDC Loan Corporation offers

affordable loans to small businesses through local financial institutions.

In 2003, EDC honored 34 businesses and organizations with the Cornerstone Award for their positive contributions to the development of the city. Honorees ranged from large corporations to retail centers to historic districts and community groups. Together they funneled more than $738 million into the Kansas City economy and added or conserved some 9,700 jobs.

One such project was the relocation of NovaStar Financial's corporate headquarters, and 240 jobs, to Kansas City, Missouri. NovaStar is a rapidly growing residential mortgage lender with $8.4 billion in loans under management as of the first quarter of 2004.

Under the EDC umbrella, several affiliated agencies operate to focus development efforts in key sectors. These agencies include the Downtown Economic Stimulus Authority of Kansas City (DESA), the Greater Downtown Development Authority (GDDA), the Land Clearance for Redevelopment Authority (LCRA),

the Tax Increment Financing (TIF) Commission, and the Port Authority of Kansas City. Together they work to curb blight; issue bonds; prepare redevelopment plans; renovate properties; build and operate city-owned public improvements; and more.

The 18th and Vine Historic District, the first phase of which received a 2003 Cornerstone Award, is a major redevelopment project that benefits from just such coordinated efforts. The 95-acre district has been the focus of restoration efforts since 1997, when the Kansas City Jazz Museum and the Negro Leagues Baseball Museum opened there and renovation of the Gem Theater was completed. A four-phase residential and economic revitalization is currently under way in the district.

Downtown Kansas City is looking forward to the biggest redevelopment effort in decades, which will involve a new 18-story headquarters for tax services provider H&R Block and a seven-block entertainment, retail, and residential district, to be called "Kansas City Live!" EDC's TIF

Commission is playing a key role with nearly $400 million in tax increment financing over a 23-year period.

Another major project for EDC now in the planning stages is the transformation of 855 acres at the former U.S. Air Force Richards–Gebaur Air Reserve Station, in south Kansas City, into an industrial park and international trade processing center. The industrial, commercial, and intermodal shipping facilities envisioned for the site are likely to attract more than $500 million in investments and create as many as 4,000 new jobs, according to estimates.

For additional information, visit the Web site of the Economic Development Corporation of Kansas City, Missouri, at www.edckc.com.

Top left: By day and night, Kansas City, Missouri's Country Club Plaza offers world-class shopping, dining, entertainment, hotels, and services in a graceful setting of Spanish architecture and European artwork. Top right: As seen from the BMA Tower, Kansas City's downtown skyline evokes the city's proud history and speaks to its shining future. Above: For the near future, exciting plans are under way for downtown Kansas City's new $250 million Sprint Center Arena (shown in this computer model). The arena will be a vital addition to the "Kansas City Live!" entertainment, retail, and residential district.

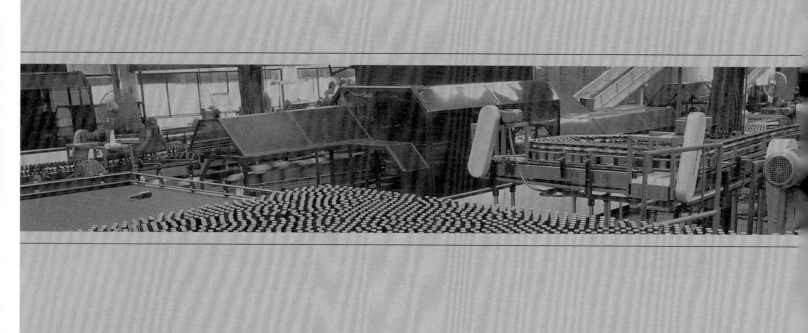

AGRIBUSINESS, FOOD PROCESSING, AND CONSUMER FOODS

ANHEUSER-BUSCH COMPANIES, INC.

A longtime innovative powerhouse in the manufacturing industry, Anheuser-Busch Companies, Inc., is also a generous and responsible corporate citizen and a leading environmental advocate.

St. Louis is the birthplace of Anheuser-Busch and the location of its corporate headquarters. The company's St. Louis brewery includes several buildings, such as the Brew House (below), that have been designated National Historic Landmarks.

St. Louis is the birthplace and world headquarters of Anheuser-Busch Companies, Inc., one of Missouri's biggest enterprises. True to one definition of the word *enterprise,* the Bavarian Brewery—the business that would eventually become Anheuser-Busch—was established in 1852 in a city crowded with breweries. After eight years, it ranked only 29th among 40 breweries in St. Louis. However, due in large measure to initiative— a synonym for *enterprise*—Anheuser-Busch has grown to become the world's leading brewer, in terms of worldwide annual volume of more than 129 million barrels produced.

REVOLUTIONIZING THE INDUSTRY

A series of remarkable leaders built the company through innovation, foresight, and an unwavering commitment to quality. The first of these was Adolphus Busch, who went to work for his father-in-law, Eberhard Anheuser, at the Bavarian Brewery in 1864. By 1869, Adolphus Busch was a full partner. And he was the first in the brewing industry to recognize that four technological developments in the second half of the 19th century— pasteurization, artificial refrigeration, refrigerated railcars, and the creation of a national railroad system—made it possible to create a national market for beer. Applying this insight, Adolphus Busch revolutionized the brewing industry, making it a national rather than a local business.

In 1876, to capitalize on this new market, Busch introduced Budweiser, a lighter, more flavorful style of beer that would become America's first national beer. Budweiser has since become the world's best-selling beer and one of its most valuable trademarks.

Anheuser-Busch also brews Bud Light, the number-one beer in sales in the United States. In fact, one out of every two beers sold

in the United States is an Anheuser-Busch product.

The company makes 30 brands of beer at its 12 breweries in the United States, including its flagship brewery in St. Louis, and others in the United Kingdom and China. Anheuser-Busch also has ownership or license agreements with brewers in Asia, Central and South America, and Europe.

While its production and sales have grown, Anheuser-Busch has never faltered from its commitment to quality and innovation. Throughout the years, the company has refused to take shortcuts in its brewing process and uses no artificial ingredients. In fact, Anheuser-Busch grows much of its own hops and barley and closely monitors materials supplied by others to ensure that only the finest ingredients are used to brew its beers.

Always an innovator, in 1950, Anheuser-Busch became the first brewer to sponsor a national television show and created a string of memorable marketing campaigns, starting with "Pick a Pair" and including "This Bud's For You" and "Whassup?!"

ENVIRONMENT, FAMILY, AND COMMUNITY MATTERS

While beer is the company's major business, Anheuser-Busch is also involved with responsible packaging, environmental stewardship, and theme parks.

Anheuser-Busch is one of the largest manufacturers in the nation, and the world's largest recycler of aluminum beverage containers. The company's 11 can and lid facilities produce 25 billion cans and 29 billion lids annually. Anheuser-Busch recycles more than 100 percent of the number of beer cans it ships domestically. The company also produces glass bottles at a plant near Houston, Texas, for use by the Anheuser-Busch brewery in Houston.

For family fun, the company's Busch Entertainment Corporation (BEC) operates nine theme parks in the United States, including Busch Gardens (in Tampa, Florida, and Williamsburg, Virginia) and SeaWorld (in Orlando, Florida; San Antonio, Texas; and San Diego, California). The Anheuser-Busch track record for innovation extends to its Discovery Cove

theme park in Orlando, the only reservations-required park of its kind offering interaction with marine life, which makes for an uncrowded experience.

Preserving and protecting the environment, promoting responsible consumption of its products, and supporting the communities in which it does business also are integral to Anheuser-Busch's operations. Hand in hand with the animal and marine-life themes at Busch Gardens, SeaWorld, and Discovery Cove, BEC is a world leader in environmental efforts. Since 1995, BEC has rescued more than 5,000 animals in distress with the goal of rehabilitating them and returning them to the wild. In addition, BEC produces award-winning environmental education programs shown in its parks, on television, and via the Internet.

As early as the turn of the century, Anheuser-Busch supported responsible consumption of its products. In 1914, its advertising slogan was "Budweiser Means Moderation." Since 1982, Anheuser-Busch and its independent

wholesalers have invested nearly $500 million to help combat all forms of alcohol abuse.

The company's support for the community dates back to its earliest days and includes a donation of $100,000 in 1906 to assist victims of the San Francisco earthquake. Today, community support takes the form of millions of dollars donated annually to organizations involved in health care, social services, and the arts and cultural enrichment. And when disaster strikes, communities can count on Anheuser-Busch to be there. For example, the company has supplied more than 1.7 million cases of canned drinking water since 1988 to areas in distress throughout the United States.

Serving the community, promoting responsibility in the consumption of alcohol, and helping to preserve the environment are important components of the company's portfolio. As a leader in the brewing, packaging, and theme park industries for decades, Anheuser-Busch Companies, Inc., has proved that "making friends is our business."

Budweiser is the best-selling beer in the world and Bud Light is the sales leader in the United States.

Right, top: Anheuser-Busch operates a brewery in Wuhan, China, and has an ownership interest in Tsingtao, China's largest brewer. Right: Discovery Cove in Orlando, Florida— one of nine parks operated by Anheuser-Busch—is unique in the theme park industry. Guests are admitted only with reservations, to create an uncrowded experience that includes interaction with marine life.

ANDY'S SEASONING, INC.

With its top quality ingredients and creative recipes, this family-owned maker of seasoned salt and breadings has become a multimillion-dollar enterprise, one of the top 25 African-American businesses in the St. Louis area, and a dedicated supporter of charitable and community causes.

Katherine Anderson is the co-founder, owner, and president of Andy's Seasoning, Inc. She has been recognized by numerous organizations for her outstanding business achievements and generous community philanthropy.

"Quality First" is the motto of Andy's Seasoning, Inc., a multimillion-dollar, family-owned and -operated company in St. Louis that produces quality seasoning and breading products.

Andy's began in 1981 in the basement of Katherine and Reuben "Andy" Anderson's home, where Reuben combined a love for cooking with a knack for blending ingredients. Through trial and error, they perfected their first product,

barbecue sauce, which Reuben sold to local grocery stores. In 1983, with the introduction of a variety of seasoned breadings, the business evolved into a full-time operation. Andy's discontinued the barbecue sauce in 1990.

When Reuben died in 1996, Katherine continued running the business. Her perseverance and strong business ethics paid off—sales increased and Andy's amassed a reputation for on-time deliveries, competitive prices, and prompt payment of suppliers.

Andy's product line includes seasoned salt; two varieties of chicken breading, Regular and Hot 'n' Spicy; several varieties of fish breading, including mild, spicy, and low sodium; a vegetable breading mix; and a tempura seafood batter mix. The recipes use select blends of premium seasonings and exotic spices that enhance the natural flavors of chicken, fish, pork, and vegetables.

Andy's provides custom-blended batters and breadings to Keystone Foods L.L.C. and Tyson Foods, Inc. The company's seasoned salt and breading mixes are sold under the Andy's brand name at grocery stores in 41 states.

Andy's helps support many charities and community groups, including the United Way, Habitat for Humanity, the St. Louis Gateway Classic Sports Foundation, the Annie Malone Children and Family Service Center, and the United Negro College Fund.

In 2000, the St. Louis chapter of the National Association of Women Business Owners named Anderson the Distinguished Woman Business Owner of the Year, and in 2002 and 2003, Andy's was recognized as one of the top 25 African-American businesses in the St. Louis area.

"We will continue to take the business to new heights," says Katherine Anderson, owner and president, "with the same resolve that helped Reuben grow the firm from a basement operation into a thriving company."

EDUCATION

CENTRAL MISSOURI STATE UNIVERSITY

Recognized nationally and worldwide, this comprehensive public university offers over 150 areas of bachelor's and graduate study with small classes, hands-on training, education abroad, and much more.

Situated in Warrensburg, about an hour's drive southeast of Kansas City, Missouri, Central Missouri State University is a public regional institution that has gradually evolved in its role and mission to meet the needs of the state's citizens. With the motto, "Education for Service," it has provided quality postsecondary education for more than 130 years.

Central offers a liberal arts curriculum and has a statewide mission in professional applied sciences and technology. Founded in 1871, Central was originally a regional school for teacher preparation, and over the years it has become a comprehensive university offering more than 150 areas of study at the undergraduate and graduate levels. More important than the number of its courses, however, is the high quality of the regionally, nationally, and internationally known programs at

Central. Aviation, criminal justice, education, graphic arts and graphic design, industrial hygiene and safety, and industrial management are a few of the many prominent programs that draw more than 10,300 students per year to Central to pursue their education dreams.

The institution's thousands of alumni include such individuals as Dale Carnegie, author of *How to Win Friends and Influence People*; Carrie Nation, temperance movement leader; and James Evans, a developer of Cheerios. The reasons for students choosing to attend Central are many. The university is a state leader in discipline-specific accreditations, which is an external endorsement that confirms the high quality of its academic programs. Other hallmarks of Central are small class sizes, with an average student-teacher ratio of 18 to one, as well as

opportunities for personal attention from a dedicated faculty.

Central is committed to preparing students to understand and meet the needs of a diverse nation and world. Doing so means providing opportunities outside the classroom for students to advance in mind, body, and spirit. The university's Office of Student Affairs is the lead area for sponsoring programs to help students learn and develop as individuals. The office maintains a list of some 180 student organizations that students may easily join. These groups represent various interests, including academic, departmental, and honor societies; community service; cultural heritage and ethnic identities; intramural and intercollegiate athletics; religions; and the Greek system.

Central has worked diligently to maintain education at an affordable

Below: A modern training fleet of Cessna 172 airplanes provides Central Missouri State University aviation students with an opportunity to learn how to fly aboard small aircraft equipped with advanced technology. Below right: The Missouri Center for Technology Education, located in the Grinstead Building, is well equipped to train educators in the best ways to help their students learn more about technology and how it is used in the workplace.

level for its students. A combination of student fees that are competitive with other Missouri educational institutions plus opportunities for financial aid make Central an attractive option, in light of its high accreditation status. In 2003, 8,222 students received a total of more than $55 million in financial aid.

While the campus is nestled in the heart of the Midwest, it provides an international environment, with students coming to the university from all parts of the world to pursue higher education. Annually, approximately 480 students representing 65 countries help create a global and diverse campus environment.

Central is widely known for its prominence in applied sciences and human services. Its four academic colleges provide programs in applied sciences and technology, arts and sciences, business administration, and education and human services. The use of advanced technology is comprehensively applied throughout the curriculum. Because of the university's outstanding reputation,

hundreds of leading businesses, industries, school districts, and government agencies actively recruit new graduates each year. Central has a 94 percent rate of graduate job placement within six months of graduation.

Central has compiled an impressive record of instruction, scholarship, and service to Missourians. Its

2003 strategic plan, "Framework for the Future: Progress by Design," provides steps to help the university achieve its mission and long-term goals. As this plan is implemented, Central will continue to serve the people of Missouri and provide a strong link in the state's educational chain.

Above: The Maastricht Friendship Tower in the West Park area of the Central Missouri State University campus stands as a monument to friendship and international understanding. Above left: With its Gothic entrance and tower, the Administration Building is a popular campus landmark, in addition to housing offices dealing with revenue, financial aid, human resources, and more.

SOUTHWEST MISSOURI STATE UNIVERSITY

Offering more than 150 undergraduate and 43 graduate programs, this multicampus university is committed to helping students succeed in their own lives and as active citizens.

During the 2004–2005 academic year, Southwest Missouri State University (SMSU) will celebrate its centennial with a theme that appropriately describes its first 100 years: "Daring to Excel." Since its founding in 1905, SMSU has played an increasingly important role in the quality of life and economic prosperity of Springfield, southwest Missouri, and the entire state. SMSU remains the second largest university in the third largest city in the fastest growing region of the state. In the decade leading up to its centennial, much has been achieved.

- Since 1995, SMSU has more than doubled the number of graduate programs offered, from 21 to 43; many of the new programs support the health care industry in Springfield. In 2002, SMSU began its first stand-alone

doctorate program in Audiology. SMSU also offers a joint Doctorate in Educational Leadership with the University of Missouri–Columbia. With more than 3,275 graduate students, SMSU has the third largest graduate program in the state.

- In keeping with the growth of graduate programs and the increased emphasis on public service, SMSU has added special units to focus the university's resources. In 2003, the Center for Applied Science and Engineering was created, adding to established units such as the Institute for School Improvement and the Mid-America Viticulture and Enology Center.

- By fiscal year 2004, SMSU's total budget, including auxiliaries,

was $220 million, with state appropriations accounting for $77.7 million. SMSU receives more than $10 million annually in research sponsorship and more than $7 million in private donations to the SMSU Foundation. SMSU has an economic impact of about $664 million per year— $1.82 million per day— on Springfield and the surrounding area.

- In 2001, SMSU became the licensee of Ozarks Public Television (KOZK in Springfield and KOZJ in Joplin). Along with the SMSU National Public Radio station, KSMU, these stations reach more than 500,000 households, including 1.3 million people, in a 57-county area.

- In 2001, the Ozarks Public Health Institute (OPHI) was established at SMSU with a mission of addressing public health and safety issues of importance to people in the region—from smoking cessation to bioterrorism to forensic support for law enforcement.

Below: On the west mall of the campus of Southwest Missouri State University–Springfield is the newly renovated and expanded Duane G. Meyer Library, at right, with the Jane A. Meyer Carillon; at $29.6 million, this was the largest capital project in the university's history. Strong Hall, at left, and David D. Glass Hall, center, also face the John Q. Hammons Fountains, foreground. From 1993 to 2003, $156 million in renovations and new construction was completed, started, or approved at SMSU.

- In spring 2003, SMSU announced that it had been awarded the first three patents in the university's history.

- In the 10 years from 1993 to 2003, approximately $156 million in new construction and renovation projects was completed, started, or approved. Project funding of about $70.1 million was received from state capital-improvement appropriations and the remainder from federal funds, dedicated student fees, local funds, and private gifts.

Southwest Missouri State University is a multicampus metropolitan university system with a statewide mission in public affairs. The purpose of the mission is to develop an educated citizenry by focusing on five themes—professional education; health; business and economic development; creative arts; and science and the environment. There is a campuswide commitment to foster competence and responsibility in the common vocation of citizenship. The mission is integrated throughout the student experience and has received national recognition.

The 20,500 students attending SMSU are from all 114 counties in Missouri, 45 other states, and 91 foreign countries. The main SMSU campus is in Springfield, and additional campuses are in West Plains and Mountain Grove.

SMSU–Springfield is a selective-admissions, graduate-level teaching and research institution. Located on 225 acres in the heart of Springfield, it offers more than 140 degree programs and other study options.

SMSU–West Plains, founded in 1963, is a separately accredited, open-admissions campus with two-year programs. Serving seven counties in south central Missouri, it offers liberal arts, occupational, and technology programs. At the SMSU branch campus at Liaoning Normal University in Dalian, China, SMSU–West Plains offers courses leading to the Associate of Arts in General Studies, with an emphasis in business.

SMSU–Mountain Grove is the research campus in the SMSU system. It serves the grape industry for mid-America, as Cornell University serves the East Coast and the University of California–Davis, the West Coast. On the campus is the Missouri State Fruit Experiment Station, which has promoted expansion of the Missouri fruit crop industry since 1899, and the Mid-America Viticulture and Enology Center (MVEC). SMSU–Mountain Grove has a world-class research program that explores the genetic resources in grape species native to North America.

For additional information, visit the SMSU Web site at www.smsu.edu.

Top left: SMSU–Mountain Grove's Faurot Hall is a landmark building. On the left is the original structure built in 1899, now on the National Register of Historic Places; at right is the 1998 addition. Top right: At SMSU–West Plains is the $4.3 million Michael J. Lybyer Enhanced Technology Center, with state-of-the-art classrooms, laboratories, and computer center, as well as the SMSU–West Plains Center for Business and Industry Training. Above: In 2003, SMSU was awarded its first three patents. The source of one patent was polymer development using a molecular beam epitaxy machine (shown here), which can grow ultra-high-purity materials one atomic layer at a time.

MISSOURI WESTERN STATE COLLEGE

True to its founding vision, this leader in higher education is committed to the educational, economic, cultural, and social development of the students and communities it serves.

Todd T. Eckdahl, Ph.D., professor of biology at Missouri Western State College, works with student Daniel Harr in the college's DNA Sequencer Laboratory. There are many research opportunities for undergraduates at the college.

Highly regarded in the region, state, and nation, Missouri Western State College is an integral part of the Missouri state system of public higher education. Founded in St. Joseph, Missouri, in 1915 as St. Joseph Junior College, Missouri Western became a four-year institution in 1969 and a full member of the State of Missouri system in 1977. Missouri Western today is distinguished as an excellent example of the democratic tradition in education—all its students, at all stages of life, are afforded the opportunity to excel in the classroom and beyond.

To this end, Missouri Western— accredited by the North Central Association of Colleges and Schools

Commission on Institutions of Higher Education—provides traditional liberal arts and career-oriented degree programs. One-year certificates, two-year associate degrees, pre-professional transfer programs, and four-year bachelor's degrees are conferred. The Graduate Center hosts master's-level programs from affiliated institutions.

As a community leader, Missouri Western has a significant positive impact on the economy and quality of life of its surrounding communities. The college employs 550 full-time faculty and staff, making it St. Joseph's ninth largest employer, and contributes $139 million yearly to the region.

Moreover, because Missouri Western emphasizes applied learning, it nurtures successful partnerships with community organizations, agencies, and businesses. More than half of Missouri Western's students participate in applied-learning opportunities found in internships, research projects, community service, and the like. Graduate schools and employers consistently give Missouri Western and its students high marks for academic and applied success.

In 2001, Missouri Western initiated "The Western Advantage: A Five-Year Strategic Plan" to chart the future of all aspects of the college, including academic affairs and enrollment management; experiential learning and student development; information technology; and workforce development, community service, and community partnerships. "In these areas, we have good reason to be confident in our future," says college president James J. Scanlon. "With the efforts of our people and support beyond the campus, Missouri Western State College will build an excellent future."

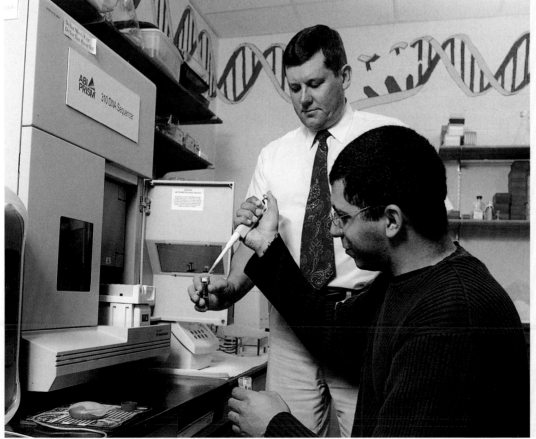

BLUE SPRINGS SCHOOL DISTRICT

Known for an outstanding curriculum and award-winning staff, this district at the eastern edge of the Kansas City metro area draws wholehearted support from both the private sector and business community.

The Blue Springs School District (BSSD) enjoys a long history as a premier learning environment. A place synonymous with quality, innovation, and tradition, it is frequently singled out for excellence.

The community demonstrates strong support. A citizens' advisory committee helps the district shape its curriculum, goals, and building projects. More than 140 businesses work with students, helping them understand and prepare for careers.

The district's close-knit neighborhood elementary schools, staffed with experienced teachers, provide a solid, challenging curriculum. A nurturing learning atmosphere pervades the 13 elementary schools and carries over to the four middle schools, where teams of teachers coordinate activities, lessons, and learning strategies for sixth through eighth graders.

Near-perfect parent attendance prevails at parent/teacher conferences. The elementary and middle schools experience almost 100 percent PTA/PTSA membership. At the two high schools, parent booster clubs provide vital support.

Activities abound at all grade levels. The high school bands participate in a variety of bowl parades, including the Rose, Orange, and Fiesta Bowls. Vocal and instrumental music, debate, and forensics students are frequent contenders for state and national titles. The district has held state championships in football, baseball, wrestling, softball, swimming, track, soccer, cross-country, cheerleading, and golf.

Seniors from both high schools annually earn more than $4 million in academic and athletic college scholarships. Each year, more than 50 seniors are recognized with state Bright Flight scholarships for scoring in the top 3 percent of the nation on the ACT assessment. Each year, the district has multiple National Merit Scholar Finalists and National Merit Commended students. Many students complete college-credit classes while in high school.

Local patrons passed a 1993 bond package that enabled the district to create a long-range technology plan, with ongoing improvements in hardware and software, that will serve BSSD students and staff well into the 21st century. Students and staff use computers and the Internet on a daily basis to gain knowledge about the world around them.

The outstanding staff of the Blue Springs schools is one of the district's hallmarks; 67 to 70 percent have advanced degrees. The district also boasts an excellent span of experience. BSSD has had one Missouri Teacher of the Year and four finalists. Three staff members have been National Disney Teachers of the Year and four have received National PTA Teacher of the Year designations. Staff members have been named State Counselor of the Year, State Administrator of the Year, and a variety of other distinctions.

Children in Blue Springs School District come to school eager and ready to learn in schools that are safe, clean, well-equipped, and well-staffed.

LINDENWOOD UNIVERSITY

This dynamic four-year liberal arts institution is renowned nationally and internationally for its dedication to excellence in higher education, its commitment to students, and its history of innovation and entrepreneurship.

Lindenwood University is distinguished for its values-based, student-centered curriculum that harks back to 1827. Named for the beautiful linden trees that grace the campus, Lindenwood is firmly rooted in two overlapping value systems: democracy and the Judeo-Christian ideal. For Lindenwood, education is the way to personal freedom and responsibility, which are the keystones of democracy. Similarly, Lindenwood's Judeo-Christian foundations include a belief in an ordered, purposeful universe; the dignity of work; the worth and integrity of every individual; the primacy of truth; and the obligations and privileges of citizenship.

Today, this 450-acre university, with more than 100 fully accredited undergraduate and graduate degree programs and nearly 12,000 students, is the geographic and academic heart of St. Charles, Missouri, a growing community located just west of St. Louis. Recognizing the educational, economic, and cultural needs of its surrounding community of 300,000 residents, Lindenwood fulfills its

responsibilities to its young students and its working-adult students. Lindenwood's consistent growth in its adult accelerated evening programs, on campus and at several satellite locations, has been phenomenal due to its reach across St. Louis. Lindenwood also features more than 30 sites throughout Missouri that offer teacher-education coursework.

Another exciting addition to Lindenwood is the Daniel Boone Home and Boonesfield Village. In 1998, the university acquired the house where Boone spent the last years of his life. With the purchase of adjacent property and with the restoration and relocation of area historic buildings, Lindenwood has created a replica pioneer town of more than 1,000

acres. The village, however, is not just a tourist destination. With Lindenwood's on-site National Center for the Study of American Culture and Values, this property is an innovative laboratory for the study of American history and the American experience, American citizenship and civics, American heritage in the arts and humanities, and much more.

Dennis Spellmann, the university's president, says, "The National Center fits right in with our mission at Lindenwood and our emphasis on entrepreneurship, citizenship, independence, and hard work. These are the same values held by Daniel Boone and his family, as well as George and Mary Sibley, founders of Lindenwood University."

The beautifully wooded campus at Lindenwood University attracts thousands of young people.

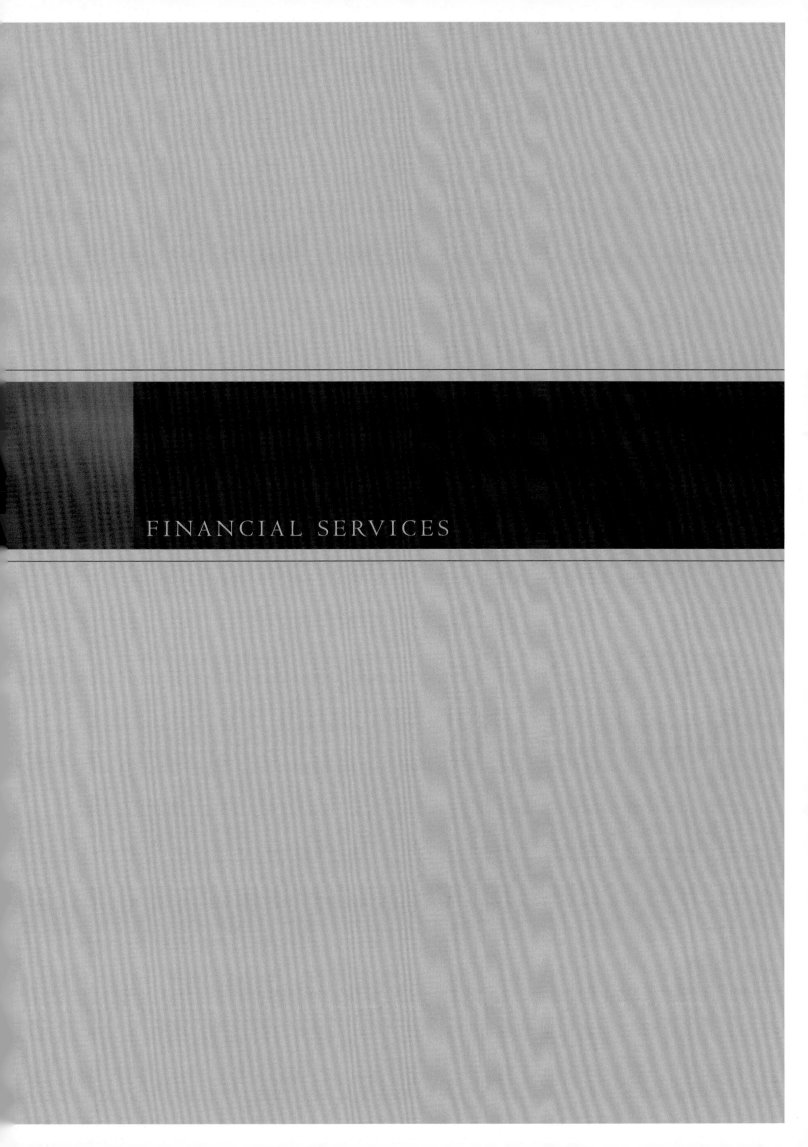

FINANCIAL SERVICES

MISSOURI CREDIT UNION ASSOCIATION

Since 1929, this association of credit unions has helped members save, obtain loans, and prepare their financial futures, combining the best of modern banking methods with the oldest key to success: serving consumers in a spirit of mutual benefit and cooperation.

The Missouri Credit Union Association, headquartered in St. Louis, also operates out of offices in Jefferson City, shown here, and Kansas City.

The Missouri Credit Union Association represents credit unions and their members in Missouri. It offers its member credit unions help with regulatory compliance, operational and technical assistance, and training for staff and volunteers.

The Missouri Credit Union Association is headquartered in St. Louis, with offices in Kansas City and Jefferson City. The association began in 1929, when 56 credit unions met in Kansas City to form what was then called the Missouri Credit Union League.

Missouri consumers have enjoyed the benefits of credit unions for more than 75 years. Credit unions are unique, not-for-profit financial institutions that are owned by the people who use them. The need for credit unions was spurred by the average citizen's inability to obtain loans from banks and other financial institutions. By joining together and sharing funds, individuals could borrow money and extend loans to their coworkers and neighbors. This "people helping people" philosophy carries on today.

By putting the interests of consumers first, credit unions can offer services such as checking, savings, and loans to their member-owners with lower fees and higher returns than can other financial institutions.

Because credit unions are not-for-profit, only members may use their services. Community-based credit unions have membership open to a particular community, which can be based on city limits, a county, or a zip code. There are credit unions based on specific businesses or select-employee groups, which serve the employees of a specific company or companies. Missouri also has many association-based credit unions, where membership is open to the people who worship in a particular church or parish, or are members of the same profession.

No matter how a credit union is formed or what the specific guidelines of its membership may be, these financial institutions benefit the entire community. Because credit unions cannot be bought or sold— they are part of the community they

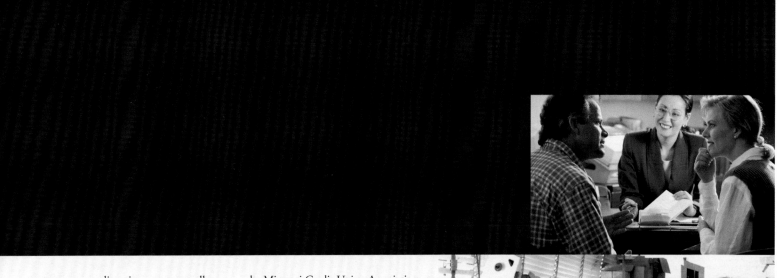

serve—credit unions are an excellent benefit for businesses to offer their employees. Together with companies, credit unions help employees save, obtain loans, and financially prepare for the future.

One of the keys to success for credit unions is to focus on individuals and their specific needs. For example, credit unions use the three C's—character, capacity, and collateral—when making loan decisions.

Character includes looking at how a person has handled past debt obligations, and helps determine the honesty and reliability of the borrower to pay debts. In reviewing a person's capacity, the credit union focuses on how much he or she can comfortably handle. And with collateral, credit unions analyze the potential borrower's assets. This careful review ensures that neither the credit union nor the member take on too much—a move that benefits both.

The association reflects the cooperative nature of credit unions. Just as credit unions work together to help members achieve their financial goals,

the Missouri Credit Union Association works with credit unions to help them meet the needs of their members.

"Credit unions serve as an important financial check-and-balance for consumers," says Rosie Holub, president and CEO of the Missouri Credit Union Association. "It is our responsibility to do everything we can to help credit unions survive and prosper."

And credit unions are certainly working to make sure their members reach financial success. Through the years, credit unions have been innovators in helping members. Direct deposit, payroll deductions, credit disability insurance, and consumer education are just a few examples. As the 21st century moves forward, credit unions are employing new ways to assist consumers through technological innovations. The Missouri Credit Union Association will be right alongside its member credit unions, helping them lead the way.

Robert Hood, who served as president and CEO of the Missouri Credit Union Association for more than 40 years, says it is easy to see

why credit unions work so well together—and work so well for members. "Our spirit of cooperation, including our willingness to share talents and knowledge, and adhering to the philosophical principles in serving members, is what makes us unique and the envy of other financial institutions."

That is the strength and the focus of Missouri's credit unions: they put people first.

Top: Credit unions are not-for-profit financial institutions owned by the people who use them. Credit unions work with member-owners to help them achieve their financial goals. Above: PC Glassworkers Credit Union board chairman Mike Hart, right, talks with coworker Gary Kidwell, a credit union member and former board director. Located in Sedalia, Missouri, PC Glassworkers Credit Union serves Pittsburgh Corning Corporation employees and their families.

GEORGE K. BAUM & COMPANY

With more than seven decades of success to its credit, this investment banking firm cultivates strong client relationships through immutable core values and solid financial advice executed with commitment, energy, innovation, and confidence.

George K. Baum & Company (GKB) has been serving clients since 1928, trading in public finance and taxable fixed income securities, and offering wealth management, investment banking, and private equity investment services. GKB keeps six core values in mind:

- the client comes first;
- growth and opportunity mean a superior return on capital;
- attracting and retaining the best people means long-term success;
- clients are served best by uncompromising standards of ethics;
- teamwork means collective talent and individual creativity; and
- the best team members balance their personal and professional lives.

GKB was founded on the eve of the Great Depression as Baum, Bernheimer & Company by George K. Baum and Earle J. Bernheimer. Baum's leadership was instrumental in helping the firm survive the economic hardships of the 1930s while maintaining a solid sales and profit record. In 1946, Baum bought out his partner, and the name officially changed to George K. Baum & Company.

Over the years, the company has enjoyed strong family leadership. G. Kenneth Baum joined his father at the firm in 1952 and dedicated more than 50 years to the company. Today, George K. Baum's grandson Jonathan E. Baum is chairman, CEO, and director of investment banking.

The company, based in Kansas City, employs 240 dedicated team members and has offices nationwide, from New York City to Seattle, Washington. The firm is recognized as one of the industry's leading underwriters of municipal bonds, working with state and local governments across the country. From 1993 to 2003, GKB served as senior manager or financial adviser for more than 2,700 municipal bond issues with a value exceeding $37 billion.

The firm also has a strong presence in investment banking, taxable fixed income trading, and wealth management. Through George K. Baum Advisors LLC, GKB provides investment banking services, mergers and acquisitions advice, and private capital raising services to middle-market business owners. The Taxable Fixed Income Group trades government, agency, and mortgage-backed securities totaling more than $6 billion annually. Through Prairie Capital Management, the firm offers innovative, customized investment advisory services to high-net-worth individuals, trusts, foundations, and companies. In addition, GKB's Merchant Banc affiliate manages a $100 million private equity fund that invests in companies in general manufacturing and business services.

GKB is well positioned to remain an independent company where team members provide clients with the best products and services while having the opportunity to work in a professionally challenging, growing, and financially rewarding environment.

Jonathan E. Baum, an alumnus of Kansas State University and the University of Chicago, and a former vice president with Salomon Brothers Inc., became chairman and CEO of George K. Baum & Company when he bought the firm from his father, G. Kenneth Baum, in 1994.

INSURANCE SERVICES

BLUE CROSS AND BLUE SHIELD OF MISSOURI

Choice and flexibility for customers is key to the success of this health care benefits company, which has served individuals and groups throughout the state for 67 years.

As a trusted partner with physicians, health care institutions, and other health care professionals, Blue Cross and Blue Shield of Missouri has served the health care coverage needs of Missouri consumers since 1936. Known for its stability and endurance in an ever-changing and challenging insurance marketplace, Blue Cross and Blue Shield of Missouri, head-quartered in downtown St. Louis, is a health care leader in 85 counties and serves nearly one million members.

The business has a strong customer-service orientation focusing on member satisfaction and quality products and services. This includes developing cooperative relationships with physicians to help them improve quality, measure results, and increase patient satisfaction, including programs such as the Physician Group Partners Program® and the Physician Consultative Committee.

"We set the highest standards for ourselves and a level of excellence unsurpassed in the industry," says Angela Braly, president and CEO.

Offering a full line of product and coverage options, Blue Cross and Blue Shield of Missouri provides consumers with choice and flexibility in meeting their health plan needs. Some benefits it offers are virtually unmatched in the industry, such as the BlueCard PPO® program, which enables members to access health care services throughout the nation.

Blue Cross and Blue Shield of Missouri is a name that both customers and the public can trust. By supporting a core of financial integrity and operational control, the company's associates have delivered consistent, stable performance. This long tradition as a Blue Cross and Blue Shield Plan has been extremely important to the continued success of the business. For

example, it has been offering Medicare Supplement plans to its valued senior customers since the 1960s.

Effective use of technology enables the company to achieve rapid and effective responses to changing customer needs. Web-based tools allow members to check the status of a claim or look for a network physician in their area by using the Internet. Physicians also have online access to the latest information, resulting in timesaving and enhanced communications.

The company is a community leader through its sponsorship of charitable events, and associates donate thousands of hours each year to volunteer efforts.

Blue Cross and Blue Shield of Missouri associates take their commitments to members, the community, and fellow associates very seriously. In working to improve accessibility to and affordability of health care services and coverage, the company's associates look forward to serving members with innovative programs and services well into the future.

Meeting with Angela Braly (center), president and CEO of Blue Cross and Blue Shield of Missouri, are Kathy Zorica, general manager of consumer services, and Dale Schulz, director of information technology.

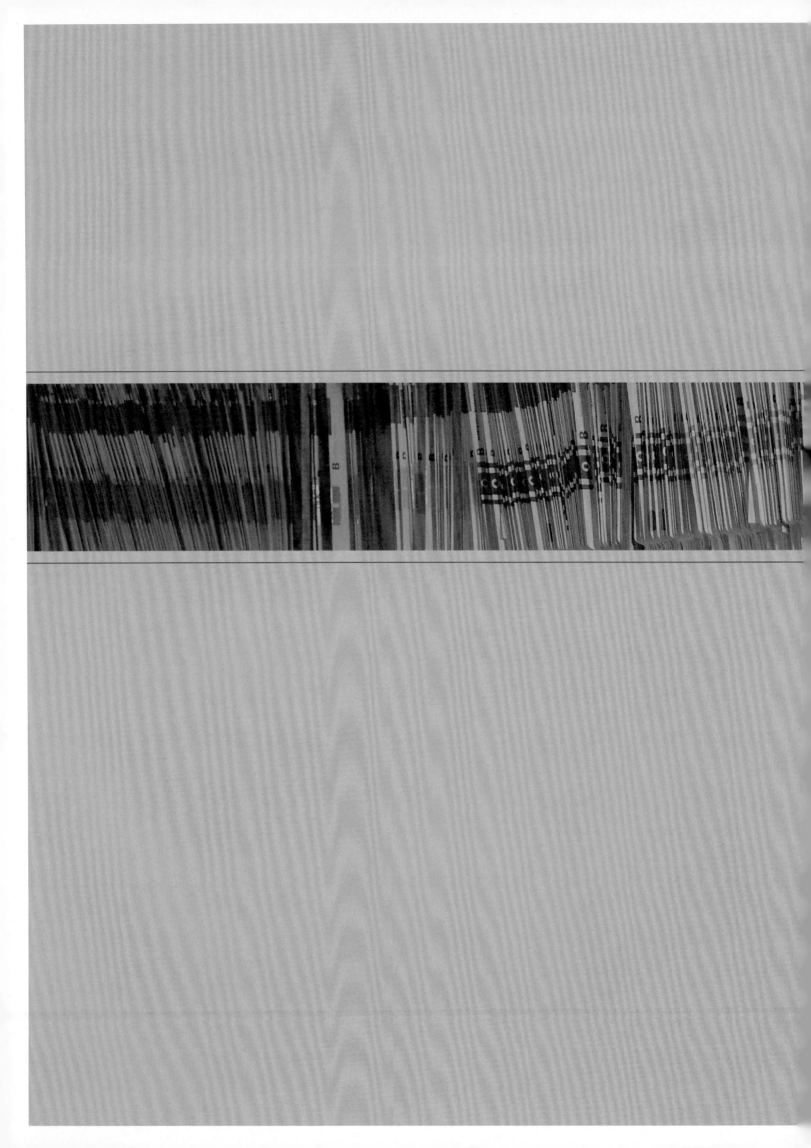

HEALTH CARE, MEDICAL SERVICES, AND MEDICAL CENTERS

MISSOURI HOSPITAL ASSOCIATION

With nationally recognized, award-winning facilities all across the state, from Cape Girardeau to St. Joseph to Kansas City to St. Louis, Missouri hospitals offer world-class health care, contribute significantly to the state's financial well-being, and offer aid and comfort during emergencies.

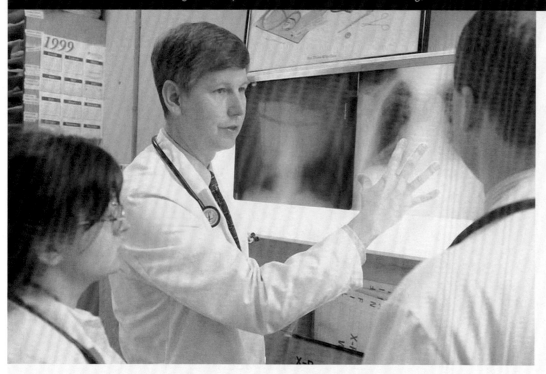

Missouri's award-winning hospitals consistently rank among the nation's best. Here, an assistant professor of clinical medicine discusses treatment options with resident physicians at one of the state's teaching hospitals.

With state-of-the-art facilities and a dedicated and skilled workforce, Missouri's 141 hospitals offer world-class health care. Year after year, the state's hospitals are recognized as among the nation's best.

Between 2000 and 2003, hospitals in the Missouri communities of Branson, Cape Girardeau, Columbia, Hannibal, Joplin, Kansas City, Springfield, St. Joseph, St. Louis, and Washington received state and national quality awards. Such recognition included Solucient's 100 Top Hospitals rating; the Missouri Quality Award, given by the Excellence in Missouri Foundation; *U.S.News & World Report*'s Best Hospitals 2003 award; *Money* magazine's acknowledgment for top hospitals in the nation; a Distinguished Hospital Award for Clinical Excellence™ from HealthGrades, Inc.; and a 2003 MissouriPRO Quality Award.

Missouri also has the distinction of being home to two of the three health care organizations in the nation to receive the prestigious Malcolm Baldrige National Quality Award. St. Louis–based SSM Health Care received the award in 2002, and Saint Luke's Hospital of Kansas City received the award in 2003.

At the same time that they are providing compassionate and quality care, Missouri's hospitals also contribute significantly to the state's economic health. In 2002, Missouri hospitals employed 130,000 employees, with a total payroll of $4.4 billion and benefits of $913 million.

Missouri's hospitals have a history of looking toward the future and working together on long-term, broad-based solutions to local, state, and national health care issues. As a result, the state's hospitals have developed innovative approaches to

- providing care to the uninsured and underinsured;
- recruiting and retaining health care workers;

- preparing for disasters or terrorist attacks in the wake of September 11, 2001;
- providing information about hospital quality to consumers; and
- building healthier communities through better management and prevention of chronic diseases.

A driving force in the rising cost of health care is the expense borne by all citizens in helping care for the uninsured. In Missouri, hospitals pay a tax known as the federal reimbursement allowance to help finance the state's Medicaid program. As a result of hospital support, Missouri moved from almost last among the 50 states in caring for the uninsured during the 1960s through the 1980s to seventh best from 1999 through 2001.

Like hospitals across the nation, Missouri health care providers face shortages of nurses and other health care professionals. As aging baby boomers place more demands on the health care system, the state's hospitals are preparing by offering significant scholarship opportunities, and forming partnerships with businesses and

educational institutions to promote health care jobs and increase the number of health care education programs.

Missouri hospitals, working with the state, have taken the lead in ongoing emergency- and disaster-preparedness planning following the terrorist attacks of September 11th. Among these efforts have been the implementation of a statewide emergency communications system, the first of its kind in the nation, and a model mutual aid agreement developed by metropolitan St. Louis hospitals.

A primary consideration for anyone who needs hospital care is the quality of that care. In Missouri, hospitals are voluntarily providing consumers with specific information about the quality of care. Metropolitan Kansas City hospitals led the way by issuing a report in 2003 with statistics about each hospital's care for patients with heart attacks, heart failure, and pneumonia. Each Kansas City–area hospital's performance rating is available on-line. In 2004, the same data for many other Missouri hospitals became available online as well.

Preventing and managing chronic illnesses is key to creating healthier communities. Recognizing this, Missouri hospitals work with other community organizations to promote health and wellness through innovative partnerships and grant programs.

Missouri's hospitals are valuable community assets, providing outstanding care to the sick and injured, serving as a source of secure and rewarding jobs, and offering a safe haven in times of emergency.

To learn more, visit the Missouri Hospital Association's Web site at www.mhanet.com and its workforce Web site at www.mohealthcareers.com.

A skilled and dedicated workforce provides state-of-the-art care to patients in Missouri's 141 hospitals. Here, a pediatric emergency nurse at a children's hospital holds one of her patients.

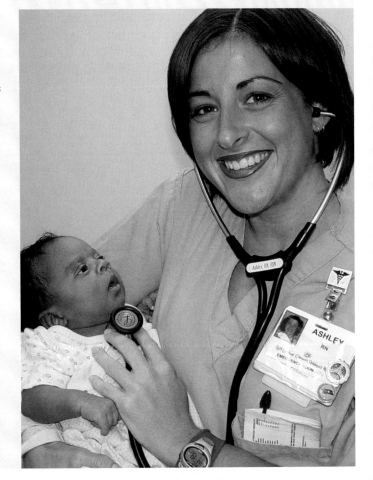

SAINT LUKE'S HEALTH SYSTEM

This well-regarded regional health care system includes Saint Luke's Hospital—Kansas City's only winner of the Malcolm Baldrige National Quality Award—plus eight additional hospitals, multiple physician practices, and home care and hospice services, and offers high quality, compassionate care.

Saint Luke's Health System is creating a new landscape for health care in Kansas City. Saint Luke's excels in building community health while delivering innovative and compassionate care to the people of its communities.

Saint Luke's commitment to Kansas City began in 1885, when All Saints Hospital, the predecessor to Saint Luke's Hospital of Kansas City, was founded. Saint Luke's Hospital is the flagship of a regional health care system that includes nine hospitals, multiple physician practices, home care and hospice, and a full range of additional health care services.

GROWING WITH KANSAS CITY

Anyone living in Kansas City is near Saint Luke's quality health care services.

Saint Luke's Hospital, one of the largest hospitals in Kansas City, is a tertiary care facility with physicians representing nearly 60 medical specialties.

Saint Luke's Mid America Heart Institute is widely recognized as one of the finest cardiac facilities in the world. Its women's cardiac center is among the top centers in the nation, and the cardiovascular clinical research center conducts leading research into drugs and new medical technology.

Saint Luke's Mid America Brain and Stroke Institute is among the top stroke centers in the nation. Its physicians and staff have earned recognition worldwide for their clinical expertise and patient outcomes.

Saint Luke's provides comprehensive obstetric services, including a neonatal intensive care unit offering the highest level of care available, according to national standards.

Saint Luke's Cancer Institute includes inpatient and outpatient care, screenings, and early detection services.

An active center of medical education and research, Saint Luke's is a primary teaching hospital for the University of Missouri–Kansas City School of Medicine, and also features Saint Luke's College of Nursing, which recently celebrated its 100th anniversary.

Saint Luke's Northland Hospital has two campuses in Kansas City's Northland region. The Barry Road campus provides medical and surgical care, intensive care, outpatient services, emergency care, a maternity center, and more. An expansion is under way that will nearly double the hospital's size. The Smithville campus is the oldest hospital in the Northland. Urgent care and emergency services, rehabilitation, behavioral health, and home care are just some of the services available.

Saint Luke's South, in Overland Park, is among the busiest hospitals in Johnson County. Saint Luke's Mid

A nurse in the coronary care unit at Saint Luke's Hospital visits with a patient. Saint Luke's Health System's nursing staff helps set the standard for quality care in Kansas City.

America Heart Institute offers cardiac intervention services at the hospital. Saint Luke's South also offers cardiovascular diagnostic testing and rehabilitation; surgical services; diabetes, sleep, and maternity centers; and more.

For more than a century, **Crittenton Behavioral Health** has cared for the emotional health of children and families. This multifaceted psychiatric organization provides prevention programs, outpatient counseling, day treatment, and residential care. It also operates outpatient clinics throughout the area.

Saint Luke's Home Care Services offers superb care and compassion, including skilled nursing, home medical equipment, and Kansas City's oldest hospice. And **Saint Luke's Medical Group** has numerous offices that house physicians who deliver Saint Luke's quality care to families across Kansas City.

Cabot Westside Health Center is one of Kansas City's leading providers of quality, culturally sensitive, bilingual primary health and education services, regardless of ability to pay. Cabot

reached another milestone in its nearly 100-year history when it broke ground in 2003 for a new facility.

Outside the metropolitan area, one finds the same quality care at **Wright Memorial Hospital** in Trenton, Missouri; **Hedrick Medical Center** in Chillicothe, Missouri; **Anderson County Hospital** in Garnett, Kansas; and **Cushing Memorial Hospital** in Leavenworth, Kansas. Saint Luke's will also open a full-service hospital in the Kansas City suburb of Lee's Summit in 2006.

A QUALITY HEALTH CARE LEADER
Saint Luke's Hospital has received numerous accolades for the quality of its care, including the Malcolm Baldrige National Quality Award. Saint Luke's is one of only two hospitals ever to win the prestigious honor, and it is the only Kansas City–based organization to win. In addition, Saint Luke's has repeatedly received the Consumer Choice Award for best hospital in Kansas City, has won three Missouri Quality Awards, and received the MissouriPRO Quality Award. Saint

Luke's was also listed among the top 50 U.S. hospitals by *Modern Maturity* magazine. Saint Luke's Health System has received many honors and was recognized by the Kansas City *Business Journal* as one of the best places to work in Kansas City because of its commitment to diversity.

"While these awards are a wonderful acknowledgment for our staff and physicians, the real value of these honors is knowing that we are being recognized for providing the very best care to the people we serve," says G. Richard Hastings, president and CEO of Saint Luke's Health System. "We're proud that our commitment to healing and heritage of compassion have helped make Kansas City a healthier place for all of us."

Top: Saint Luke's Health System is committed to staying on the leading edge of health care by utilizing state-of-the-art technology and performing breakthrough research that help improve clinical outcomes. Bottom: The first phases of Saint Luke's East–Lee's Summit will be completed in 2005, including ambulatory surgery, diagnostic imaging, emergency care, and offices for physicians. A full-service hospital will open in 2006.

SOUTHEAST MISSOURI HOSPITAL

Taking the lead in innovative health care, 269-bed Southeast Missouri Hospital continues to advance, adding state-of-the-art technologies and sweeping renovations while strengthening its long-standing commitment to community wellness.

Founded in 1928 by civic-minded physicians and businessmen, Southeast Missouri Hospital, the region's preeminent health care organization, has evolved from a small, 90-bed hospital to a 269-bed medical center that annually serves almost 100,000 inpatients and outpatients from 22 counties.

At the hospital's corporate base is the Southeast Missouri Hospital Association, which consists of nearly 800 community members. The association elects the board of trustees, the hospital's governing body.

In addition to five regionally recognized centers of excellence—the Regional Heart Center, Regional Cancer Center, Regional Brain and Spine Center, Emergency Services, and Center for Women's and Children's Services—the hospital, staffed by more than 250 physicians and 1,700 employees, offers a full continuum of health care and wellness services.

A LEADER IN CARE

Over the years, Southeast has brought many advances in care and technology to the region. During 2004 alone, the Regional Cancer Center at Southeast became the first cancer center in southeast Missouri and one of just 50 cancer centers worldwide to offer Novalis® Shaped Beam Surgery™. Novalis offers unsurpassed precision in treating certain cancers, including those of the brain, spine, and prostate.

Another recent addition to the cancer center is a Varian Clinic Linear Accelerator featuring intensity-modulated radiation therapy (IMRT) to deliver high doses of radiation directly to cancer cells in a precise, targeted way.

Also in 2004, Southeast began linking its Picture Archiving and Communications System (PACS) to off-site physician offices.

At the Regional Heart Center, established nearly 6,000 heart surgeries ago in 1984, Southeast's cardiovascular surgeons are among a handful in the nation to perform 60 percent of heart bypass operations off pump; at the Regional Brain and Spine Center, neurosurgeons this year performed the region's first awake craniotomy.

A new affiliation with SSM Cardinal Glennon Children's Hospital in St. Louis means that the more than 14,000 children who rely on Southeast for pediatric services each year will have facilitated access to subspecialty services at Cardinal Glennon.

More than 70,000 babies have been born at Southeast since 1928. Its 90-member obstetrics staff is the most experienced in the region, with a combined total of 900 years of experience.

Southeast Missouri Hospital is located in the southeast portion of the state in Cape Girardeau. Southeast has been meeting the region's health care needs since 1928.

A Leader in Facilities

The opening of 40 new patient rooms at Southeast Missouri Hospital in early 2004 completed the first phase of a $16 million bed modernization project, which continues with a sweeping renovation of six other existing patient care units. When the modernization project is completed in 2005, 67 percent of Southeast's patient rooms will be private.

On the main hospital campus, progress continues on a new $15 million medical office building also slated for completion in 2005. The building will house office space for 40 physicians and services for patients, including radiology and laboratory services and a retail pharmacy.

Southeast's investment in community health is a long-standing one that began with the establishment of the region's first hospital-based wellness center in 1979. In summer 2004, just blocks from its main campus, Southeast will open HealthPoint Plaza, a new, medically based fitness and rehabilitation center. Southeast also launched HealthWorks in 2004, a program that helps businesses manage and track employee wellness.

A Leader in Nursing

At a time when agency nurses, shortages, and "burned out" nurses seem to be the professional norm nationally, Southeast looks to a positive future. Both nurse and patient satisfaction levels are much higher at Southeast than in hospitals of similar size across the nation.

Southeast is an environment in which nurses choose to practice, as evidenced by a less than 4 percent staff vacancy rate compared to a 10 to 12 percent rate nationwide. Of the present staff, the average number of years employed at Southeast is 10. And of Southeast's nearly 600 nurses, 94 percent are RNs and 23 percent are certified in their specialty.

Southeast is also among the best in the nation in terms of patient satisfaction, according to the National Research Corporation's (NRC+Picker) Group, an independent patient-opinion survey organization that reviews and tabulates Southeast's patient satisfaction results. When asked to rate their care, over 97 percent of Southeast's patients said it was either "good", "very good", or "excellent", with more than 57 percent giving the hospital an "excellent" rating. Those results place Southeast above the 95th percentile when compared to the care ratings of more than 600 other NRC+Picker client hospitals.

A Leader in the Community

Southeast helps meet the region's ongoing need for health care professionals through its College of Nursing and Health Sciences.

The hospital's innovative Generations Center is a community education resource, and Southeast's award-winning Web site— www.southeastmissourihospital.com— provides 6,000 pages of valuable information about hospital services and health matters that extend Southeast's regional medical center expertise worldwide.

Above: More than 1,300 babies are born each year at Southeast Missouri Hospital, a recognized regional leader in obstetrics care. Above left: Novalis® Shaped Beam Surgery™, now available at Southeast's Regional Cancer Center, is considered the most sophisticated approach to stereotactic radiosurgery and radiotherapy available today.

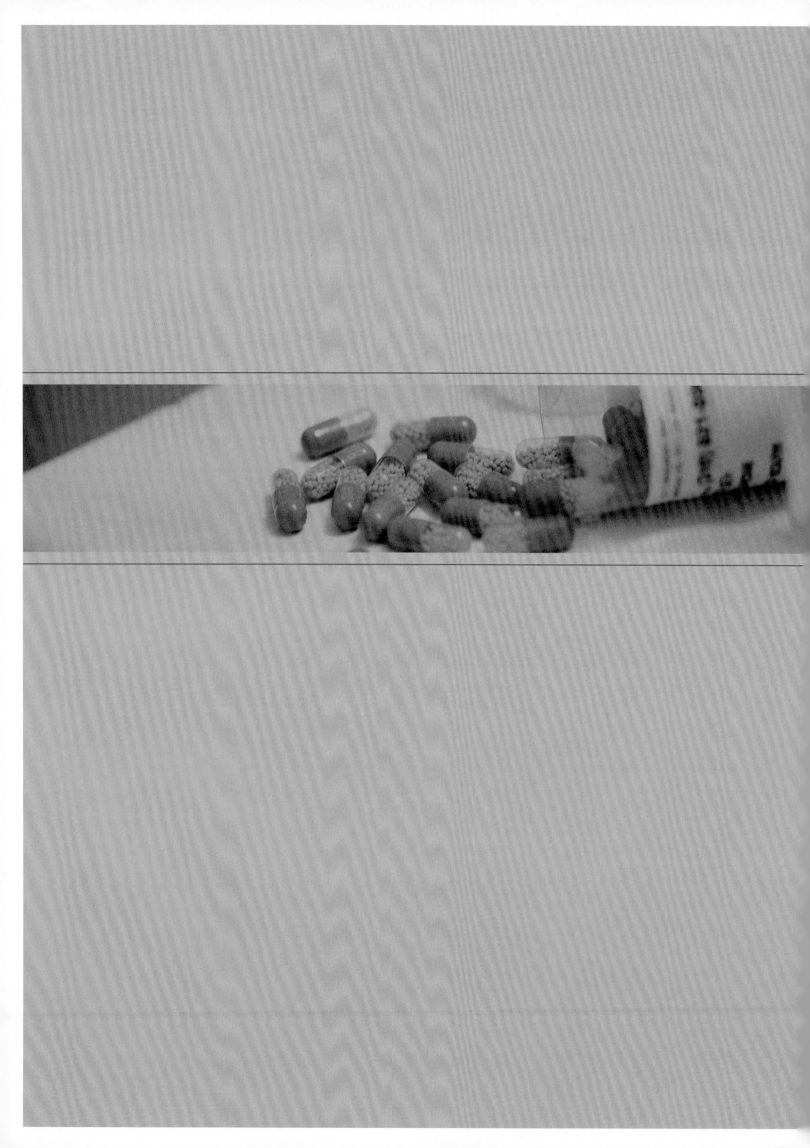

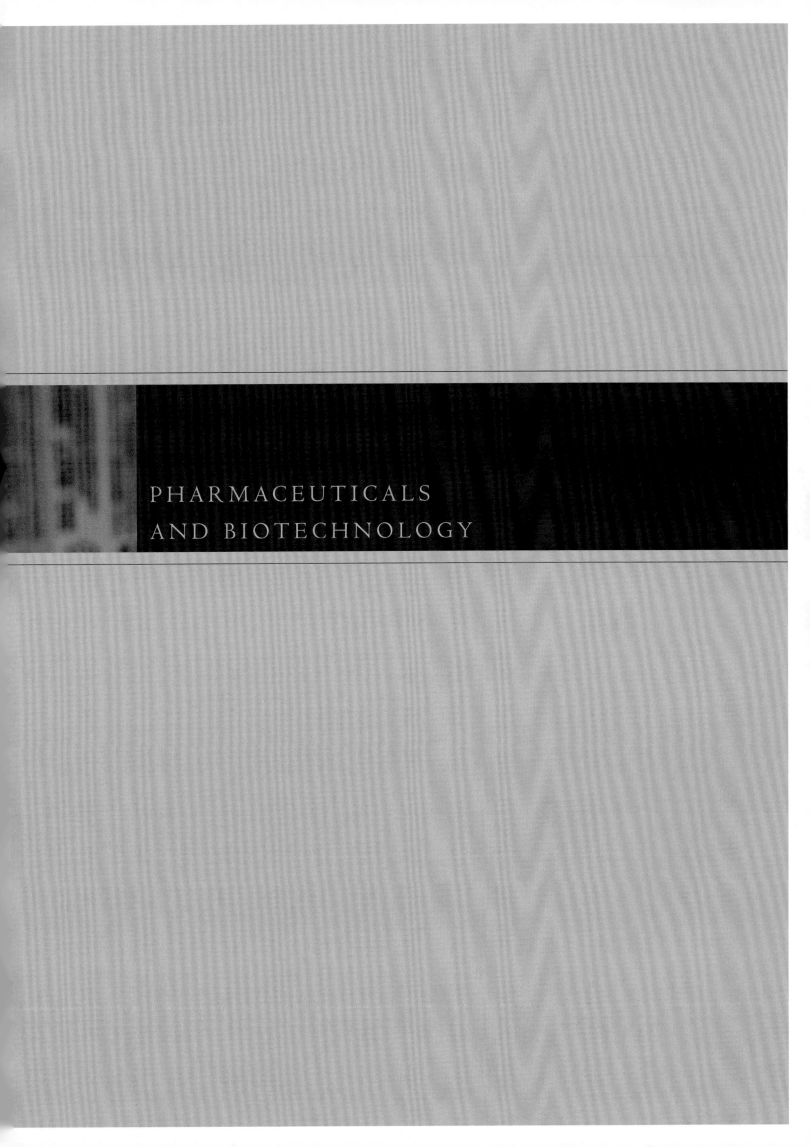

PHARMACEUTICALS
AND BIOTECHNOLOGY

EXPRESS SCRIPTS

This pharmacy benefit manager, one of North America's largest, succeeds through pursuing a rigorous agenda of pertinent, unbiased research; building collaborative relationships with clients; and ensuring that members receive convenient and affordable pharmaceutical care.

In 2003,
Express Scripts
processed more than

410 million medications
for more than

50 million patients
in North America.

EXPRESS SCRIPTS®

www.express-scripts.com

Express Scripts' state-of-the-art ability to accurately and safely process a high volume of prescriptions and medications ensures the reduced cost of prescription drugs—a great benefit for the company's members and customers.

Since its inception in 1986, when the pharmacy benefit management (PBM) industry was in its infancy, Express Scripts has had a mission: to reduce the cost of prescription drugs. As a PBM, Express Scripts helped organize the pharmaceutical supply chain, increasing the efficiency of drug distribution, managing costs in the pharmacy benefit, and improving health outcomes and satisfaction for its members.

Express Scripts differentiates itself in the marketplace through its:

• independence and integrity
• knowledge and innovation
• client focus
• service excellence.

Express Scripts performs a number of important functions that its patients never see—functions that make vital medications available to them at an affordable cost and help protect their safety. Express Scripts secures discounts from drug manufacturers and pharmacy retailers, helps plan sponsors and their patients take advantage of those discounts, encourages the use of more

We help **make** the use of prescription drugs **safer** and more **affordable** for **Americans**

economical generic drugs and mail delivery, and promotes the appropriate use of prescription drugs. At every point, the interests of Express Scripts are fully aligned with those of its plan sponsors and their patients.

Express Scripts began in St. Louis as a joint venture between Sanus Corp. Health Systems and a retail chain of more than 100 pharmacies. Express Scripts was purchased by New York Life Insurance Company in 1989 and became a publicly traded company

(Nasdaq: ESRX) in 1992. Express Scripts experienced tremendous growth through expansion of its client base and product lines. The company soon became a leader in progressive health care management by delivering advanced capabilities in four complementary health care markets. By 1998, Express Scripts employed more than 1,500 employees.

Express Scripts has also grown through several acquisitions: ValueRx; National Prescription Administrators,

Inc. (NPA); and Diversified Pharmaceutical Services (DPS).

Today, Express Scripts employs more than 8,500 people nationwide, with its corporate headquarters located in St. Louis. The company also maintains major sites in Tempe, Arizona; Orlando, Florida; Farmington Hills, Michigan; Bloomington, Minnesota; Albuquerque, New Mexico; East Hanover, New Jersey; Troy, New York; and Philadelphia and Harrisburg, Pennsylvania.

INFORMATION TECHNOLOGY,
COMMUNICATIONS, AND THE MEDIA

CHARTER COMMUNICATIONS, INC.

More than a cable television company, this pioneer in digital and broadband communications delivers video programming, high-speed Internet access, digital cable, video-on-demand, high-definition television (HDTV), and interactive services.

Charter Communications, Inc.'s future-forward cable infrastructure (which includes a combination of fiber-optic lines and coaxial cables) and the company's broadband infrastructure (which enables high-speed access to information and communications networks) provide customers with the complete range of products and services.

Founded in 1993, Charter Communications, Inc., is among the top broadband companies in the United States.

Charter (Nasdaq: CHTR) serves 6.3 million customers in 37 states and employs 15,500 people nationwide. Founded as an analog cable television company, Charter now provides customers with access to the latest digital and broadband communication and entertainment technology.

Years ago, Paul Allen—chairman of Charter and co-founder of Microsoft Corporation—envisioned a "Wired World," a global broadband network that would interconnect every home and facilitate the convergence of television, computers, the Internet, and communications. Charter is achieving that vision by developing and deploying advanced interactive services through its broadband infrastructure. "In our view, the broadband network infrastructure built by the U.S. cable industry is second to none, and we're proud to say that Charter is a major force within cable's broadband transformation," says Carl Vogel, Charter president, CEO, and director.

Charter has worked hard to build the network that allows the company to deliver advanced products and services. Charter has upgraded its cable infrastructure to a state-of-the-art combination of fiber-optic lines and coaxial cable. This broadband infrastructure enables high-speed, always-on access

to a rich information and communications network. For customers, this means an expanded choice of video programming, high-speed Internet access, digital cable, video-on-demand, high-definition television (HDTV), interactive services, and other exciting products and services the future may bring.

Since it began, Charter has been intent on providing high quality service, the latest technology, and a wide variety of video programming to customers at a fair price. That philosophy has not changed. As digital technology melds video, audio, and voice communications with personal computing and the Internet, Charter's goal is to make the wired world accessible to as many people as possible. Charter continues to offer competitive prices, and when customers purchase bundled services the value becomes even greater.

Charter also is proud to support its local communities through civic and charitable organizations. More than 9,000 schools benefit from

Charter's participation in the Cable in the Classroom program, which provides free cable connections and programming along with high-speed data to schools.

Charter excels in delivery of broadband service and was among the first to deploy video-on-demand. Through the end of 2003, Charter has made video-on-demand available to nearly one-third of its digital-capable homes.

Charter also is delivering on the long-awaited promise of HDTV. Charter has made the crystal-clear images and impressive visuals of HDTV available to nearly half of its digital customers, including all of the top-100 television markets it serves. The company is working in concert with high-end video equipment retailers to bring HDTV to Charter customers who already have the latest generations of HDTV equipment in their homes.

In interactive television, Charter's unique interactive service—the Charter Communications i-Channels—are available to more than one million Charter Digital Cable customers. The company's i-Channels include news, weather, sports, entertainment, shopping, money, games, customer care, and iTV Central, which offers instant access to local and national content, as well as on-demand entertainment.

"For our industry at large, and for Charter specifically, opportunities abound," Vogel says. "Our network is host to a wider and richer array of services than we have ever known, from digital television to high-definition video to video-on-demand to high-speed Internet access to digital video recording (DVR) and telephone service. The broadband revolution is beginning to stir, and Charter is thrilled to be among those leading the way."

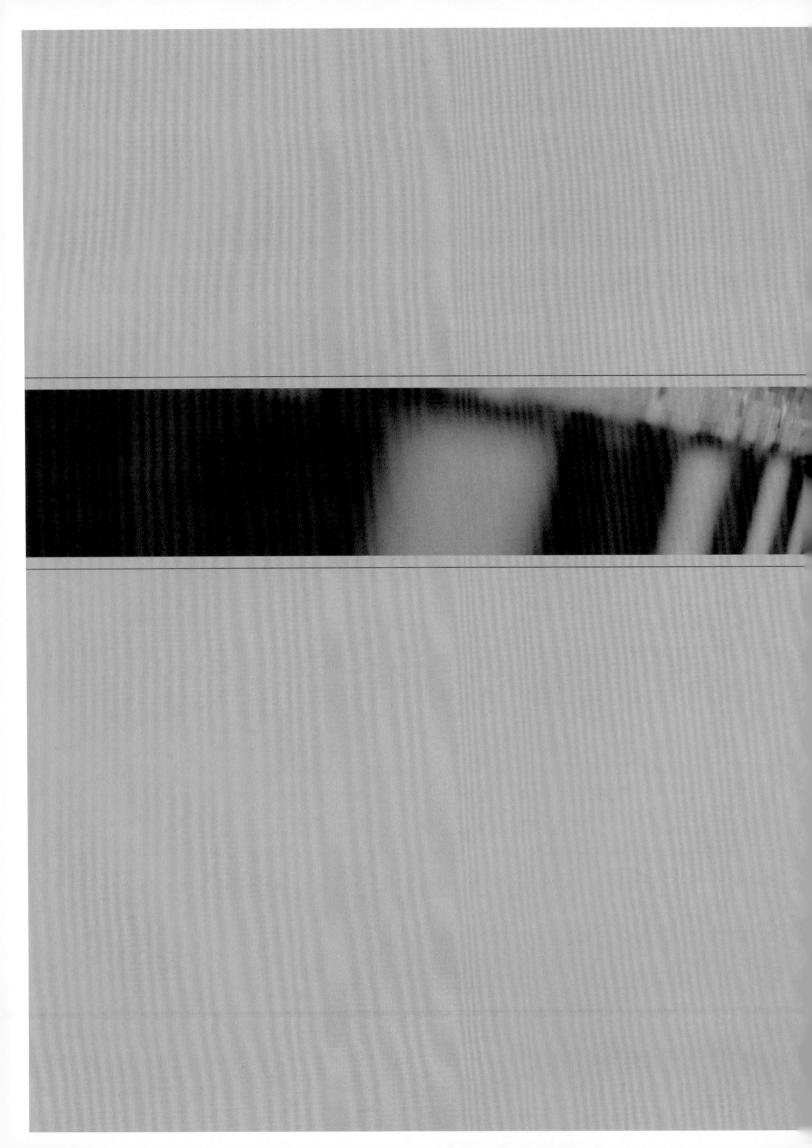

MANUFACTURING

MAVERICK TUBE CORPORATION

This independent-thinking company makes oil country tubular goods, line pipe, downhole coiled tubing, coiled line pipe, umbilicals, mechanical tubing, structural tubing, standard pipe, pipe piling, steel conduit, and pipe couplings at facilities conveniently situated for swift transport of its products to oil fields and construction sites.

To launch, develop, and sustain a traditional American manufacturing company is no mean accomplishment. But to swiftly bring a start-up enterprise to a top rank in a uniquely unforgiving industry is remarkable. Such success marks the rise of Maverick Tube Corporation, one of North America's leading producers of steel tubular products for energy and industrial applications and one of the largest producers of oil country tubular goods (OCTG) and line pipe for petroleum extraction, refining, and transport.

Headquartered in Chesterfield, Missouri, a suburb of St. Louis,

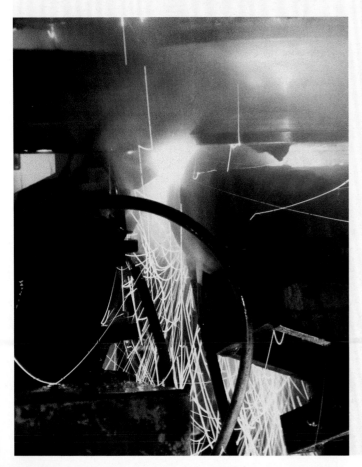

White-hot sparks fly as a Maverick Tube Corporation welder pressure-fuses a steel seam at temperatures approaching 2,000 degrees Fahrenheit.

Maverick employs some 2,600 men and women and operates 12 plants strategically located across North America—three adjacent to Nucor's steel mill in Hickman, Arkansas; another four in and around Houston, Texas; and facilities in Georgia, Ohio, Tennessee, and Michigan. A major operation in Calgary, Alberta, serves the thriving oil and gas industry of Canada's western plains, as well.

Maverick's Hickman facility houses one million square feet of state-of-the-art manufacturing space and six production lines adjacent to Nucor's premier steel mill, which is among the world's most efficient of its kind. Nucor supplies a significant amount of the approximately 1.5 million tons of steel Maverick uses annually, and their collaborative operation has been immensely beneficial to both companies. The proximate Nucor and Maverick mills can convert scrap metal from barges on the Mississippi River into finished tubing within 36 hours; pipe can be on its way to a well site within four

hours after a master coil arrives at the plant.

FROM FEISTY NEWCOMER TO INDUSTRY LEADER

Choosing a name that means independent thought and action, the company's founders launched Maverick Tube Corporation in 1978 in Union, Missouri. The company shipped its first lot of small-diameter tube—the kind used in baby furniture, bicycles, and lawn mower handles, for instance—the following year. Striving to develop an optimum product range and achieve a sustainable competitive advantage, Maverick's managers confidently grew their company through strategic expansion, constant facility improvement, and carefully timed mergers and acquisitions.

In 1980, Maverick entered the energy market with its first OCTG output, soon followed by line pipe products and additional manufacturing facilities. To finance increasingly ambitious plans for market

expansion and modernization, management took the company public in March 1991 (NYSE: MVK). Emphasizing diversification (nearly half of the products that the company manufactured in 2003 were not produced by Maverick five years earlier) and strong customer service, Maverick has justified investor confidence with rising revenue, cash flow, earnings, and equity value.

In the oil and gas sector—which generates 70 percent of Maverick's revenue—newly drilled wells are the company's primary market, followed by line pipe, which moves well output to distribution and user sites. Maverick manufactures pipe and tubes of up to 16 inches in outside diameter, a size range that accommodates 90 percent of oil and gas industry needs and about half of all line pipe applications. Offsetting the volatility of oil and gas markets, Maverick has diversified into the small-diameter steel conduits used in nonresidential construction projects to protect electrical cabling, as well as round

and square hollow structural sections for industrial applications.

Contemporary projects using Maverick's industrial products include pipe piling for the expansive new wharves at the Port of New Orleans in Louisiana; standard pipe for the mammoth "Big Dig" harbor tunnel project (officially known as the Central Artery/Tunnel Project) in Boston, Massachusetts; and hollow structural sections for the Las Vegas Eiffel Tower, the doomed vessel of the film *Titanic*, and Wal-Mart stores nationwide.

A MODEL OF MODERN MANUFACTURING

Few undertakings demand such equipment reliability and consistent performance as the oil and gas industry, where failure can be lethal as well as costly. No small part of Maverick's success lies in the superior product it delivers to oil field operators. Beginning with top quality raw materials processed by the most advanced methods, Maverick finishes all its products

Top: President and CEO Gregg Eisenberg is at the helm of Maverick Tube Corporation. Bottom: Maverick is headquartered in Chesterfield, Missouri.

MAVERICK TUBE CORPORATION

Left: Massive steel coils arrive at Maverick Tube Corporation's facility in Hickman, Arkansas.
Right: A master roll is run through a coil slitter on its way to becoming lengths of steel tubing.

in-house, exercising comprehensive control over the entire manufacturing process. Inner and outer surface quality, wall thickness uniformity, collapse and corrosion resistance, paint or coating adherence, ductility, and machinability—everything is rigorously monitored, tested, and inspected.

The welded tube manufacturing process starts with a master coil of steel, some six feet in diameter and width, which can yield up to seven slit coils. The slit coil is placed on an accumulator and welded at the ends for a continuous operation. The slit coil is then passed through forming cages that gradually roll the flat steel strip until the two outside edges meet to be welded at temperatures between 1,800 and 2,000 degrees Fahrenheit. Downline, the resulting

weld is annealed to ensure molecular integrity throughout the tube, then air cooled. The new tubing is formed through successive rolls and gradually reduced in diameter to desired specifications and finish. The tube is then cut to length, and various end finishes are applied as required. Some specialized oil country products are further worked by being passed through a quench and temper furnace to increase strength to job specification.

As part of the company's strategy of keeping production costs low, Maverick runs its plants with high line speeds and reduced downtime, a practice made possible by high levels of automation, extensive staff training, preventive maintenance to equipment, and, above all, good forecasting made possible by

close working relationships with customers.

REALITY-BASED OPTIMISM
Maverick is ideally positioned to serve its chosen markets with highly skilled, well trained, and motivated employees; sophisticated controls over all facets of manufacture for consistent quality; and facilities conveniently located near their markets with access to swift, low-cost shipping. Not surprisingly, the firm's core commitment to safety, innovation, quality, and service embraces exploration of new opportunities for growth by expansion and acquisition.

The independence of thought and action shown by Maverick's founders is still very evident today.

BIOKYOWA INC.

An exemplary economic and community partner, BioKyowa Inc.—whose state-of-the-art plant produces amino acids for nutritional food supplements and much more—was one of the first major investments by a Japanese company in the state of Missouri.

When Kyowa Hakko Kogyo Co., Ltd.—the Japanese parent company of BioKyowa Inc.—was looking worldwide for a location to build a plant for producing amino acids, it chose Cape Girardeau, Missouri, as the ideal location. The plant was built during 1982 and 1983 and was an immediate boon to the economic and employment outlook for the region. Local personnel, hired to fill supervisory positions, were sent to Japan for their training. Upon their return, they trained local operators and maintenance employees in the complex technicalities of producing amino acids (the chief components of proteins) for feed and industrial use, supplying U.S. and world markets.

COMMITMENT TO EXCELLENCE, SCHOLARSHIP, AND CULTURE

Since its beginnings, the BioKyowa facility has gone through several million-dollar expansions and added a great number of employees. The facility that started off with 50 to 60 employees and produced 2,000 metric tons per year of one feed-grade amino acid has grown into a multiple-plant facility producing high quality, value-added amino acids for products such as nutritional food supplements and as raw materials for pharmaceutical and also industrial use. Production has become ever more technically complex, and the required skill level of its 160 employees is very demanding.

BioKyowa is known as a caring corporate citizen. For example, the BioKyowa Scholarship enables children of employees to attend Southeast Missouri State University in Cape Girardeau. And BioKyowa's groundbreaking Visiting Japanese Scholar Program brings one Japanese scholar each year to the university and its Center for Faulkner Studies to conduct research with the Brodsky Collection of William Faulkner materials and participate in cultural exchanges. This program honors the special relationship that Faulkner, the American literary lion, developed with the people of Japan during his State Department visit to the country in 1955.

Kohta Fujiwara, president of the company, says, "BioKyowa Inc. upholds the American dream while celebrating the best that both the East and West have to offer to the mutual benefit of our customers, employees, and greater community."

Commitment to the protection of the environment and the safety of its employees are integral parts of BioKyowa's operating philosophy.

BAYER CROPSCIENCE

With a name synonymous with reliability, dependability, and responsibility, and a position as a world power in crop protection, biotechnology, and professional pest management, Bayer CropScience is breaking new ground with innovations in the global crop science market.

Everything at Bayer CropScience is geared toward partnership for growth: By enhancing crop yields and crop quality, the company creates value for farmers and distributors, shareholders, and partner companies as well as the entire food industry.

Its mission is to be the worldwide leader in providing innovative products and combined solutions for agriculture and environmental health. As such, the company provides crop solutions and products for the crop protection, biotechnology, and seed markets; turf and ornamental and professional pest-management markets; and consumer lawn and garden markets.

GROWING THE MARKET

Formed from a merger of Bayer Crop Protection and Aventis CropScience in 2002, Bayer CropScience benefits strongly from the experience of its predecessors and has become one of the world's leading innovative enterprises in the crop science industry. The company offers one of the most comprehensive crop protection portfolios in the world and holds top market positions in all its core business areas.

Bayer CropScience, with worldwide headquarters in Monheim, Germany, is a separate legal entity within the worldwide Bayer Group. The Bayer Group is an international research-based company with core businesses in health care, crop science, polymers, and specialty chemicals, with 115,400 employees worldwide and a portfolio of more than 10,000 products. Its stock is a component of the Deutscher Aktien Index (DAX, the German stock index) and is listed on the New York Stock Exchange (NYSE: BAY). For 2003, the Bayer Group recorded sales of 28.6 billion euros.

Worldwide, the Bayer CropScience organization employs 23,000 people in 122 countries, with global sales of $6 billion, and is organized into three areas of activity: CropScience, BioScience, and Environmental Science.

Bayer CropScience's products include many well-known brands, such as the Bayer Advanced line of home, lawn, and garden products; Premise, an insecticide for professional pest control; herbicides such as Sencor and Liberty; Folicur fungicide; and Sevin insecticide.

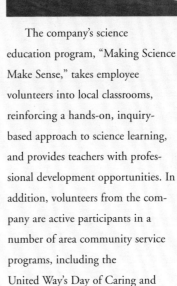

The company's loyal customers include distributors, growers, farm cooperatives, homeowners, golf course superintendents, professional pest control operators, and custom applicators.

In Partnership with Missouri

In North America, the company's business headquarters are located in Research Triangle Park, North Carolina. A manufacturing site in Kansas City, Missouri, and a research facility in nearby Stilwell, Kansas, compose the company's Core Technology Center.

In Kansas City, Bayer CropScience's crop protection activities date back to 1956, when Chemagro first began its operations at the confluence of the Blue and Missouri Rivers in northeast Kansas City. Through the years, the company changed names to Mobay, Miles, and Bayer, remaining committed to its presence in the Kansas City community.

The Kansas City site is highly automated, with more than $525 million in assets, boasting an impressive workforce that includes plant operators and maintenance technicians; engineers; chemists and other scientists; and supply chain and health, environment, and safety professionals.

The nearly 600 highly skilled and trained employees operate the facility 24 hours a day, 365 days a year, synthesizing active ingredients and formulating and packaging final products. More than 50 percent of the active ingredients produced at the site are exported.

Commitment to the Community

To ensure the safety of its neighbors and the environment, the Bayer CropScience site is equipped with a professionally trained emergency brigade and a site-based hazardous-material response team, as well as state-of-the-art waste-treatment facilities.

Beyond the company's commitment to the safety of the community, Bayer CropScience also demonstrates a strong interest in the well-being of the Kansas City community through a variety of community service, philanthropic, and stewardship activities.

The company's science education program, "Making Science Make Sense," takes employee volunteers into local classrooms, reinforcing a hands-on, inquiry-based approach to science learning, and provides teachers with professional development opportunities. In addition, volunteers from the company are active participants in a number of area community service programs, including the United Way's Day of Caring and Christmas in October.

Bayer CropScience is distinguished by its dedication to fostering new ideas and its determination to provide customers with quality, affordable products and services.

Such dedication and determination, combined with the company's drive to respond to the ever-increasing demand for agricultural efficiency, make Bayer CropScience a shining example of the spirit of enterprise in the state of Missouri and around the world.

Both pages: Bayer CropScience operates a state-of-the-art manufacturing facility in Kansas City near the confluence of the Missouri and Blue Rivers.

GENERAL MOTORS CORP.

The Wentzville Truck Assembly Center in St. Charles County is the exclusive manufacturer of GM's full-size extended passenger vans, whose upgraded safety and reliability features include vehicle stability enhancement systems (VSES), four-wheel antilock brakes, and daytime running lamps.

General Motors Corp. (GM), the world's largest vehicle manufacturer, designs, builds, and markets cars, trucks, automotive systems, heavy-duty transmissions, and locomotives worldwide. In 2003, the company (NYSE: GM) earned $3.8 billion from continuing operations on sales and revenues of $185.5 billion. However, everything GM does originates with its customers. Researching, hearing, and understanding customer needs and desires help GM define its brands.

GM invests aggressively in high technology and E-business within its global operations and through such initiatives as e-GM, GM BuyPower, OnStar, and its Hughes Electronic Corp. subsidiary. GM also operates one of the world's largest and most successful financial institutions, GMAC.

Founded in 1908, GM sells its vehicles in some 200 countries, and has manufacturing, assembly, or component operations in more than 30 countries. In the St. Louis area, more than 4,000 GM employees work in automobile manufacturing,

parts warehousing and distribution, auto and home financing, insurance, real estate, and technical training.

St. Charles County is home to one of GM's largest assembly plants, the Wentzville Truck Assembly Center. Located on 569 acres along Route A in Wentzville, the Wentzville Center is the manufacturing center for all Chevrolet Express and GMC Savana full-size vans, and the only manufacturing facility for GM's 15-passenger, full-size extended passenger vans.

About 2,500 hourly employees—represented by United Auto Workers Local 2250—and 200 salaried employees produce the vans, using 300 multitask robots and many programmable devices to monitor and control equipment and processes.

Fresh off its first major redesign in seven years, the 2003 Chevy Express and GMC Savana full-size van lineup offered an all-new look, upgraded power trains, and enhanced safety and reliability features—such as a 155-inch wheelbase, stability enhancement systems, and traction

control—plus exclusive new features designed to deliver more for the commercial user.

Highlighting a long list of what is new and improved for the model year are three industry firsts for full-size vans: all-wheel-drive models, left-side 60/40 entry/load door availability, and unique side-access doors on Express Access and Savana Pro models.

New all-wheel-drive vans have been added to the two-wheel-drive "G-model" lineup, employing a full-time viscous-coupled transfer case to offer the best on-road, wet- or dry-pavement handling traction ever engineered into a full-size van. The industry's first 60/40 left-side entry/load door, available on regular-length passenger and cargo vans, provides the segment's most flexible passenger entry/cargo loading capability. The new side-access doors with remote release on work-oriented Savana Pro and Express Access models allow access to tools and parts from both sides of the vehicle to save time and steps.

GM will begin installing vehicle stability enhancement systems (VSES) in GMC Savana and Chevrolet Express 15-passenger vans during the 2004 model year production cycle. This enhancement underscores GM's leadership in bringing this important safety technology to more customers than any of its competitors. VSES helps drivers maintain control of vehicles under difficult driving conditions such as ice, snow, gravel, wet pavement, and uneven road surfaces, as well as in emergency lane changes or avoidance maneuvers.

VSES works by recognizing wheel skid. Sensors detect the difference between the steering wheel angle and the direction the driver is actually turning by "reading" the steering wheel position, the amount of sideways force in play, the vehicle's speed, and the vehicle's response to steering-wheel input. The system then uses the brakes to enhance control of the vehicle's direction and to help keep it on course. VSES automatically reduces the engine torque and applies precise amounts of pressure to the

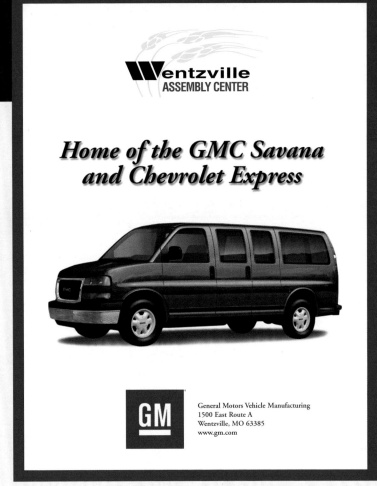

Wentzville
ASSEMBLY CENTER

Home of the GMC Savana and Chevrolet Express

GM General Motors Vehicle Manufacturing
1500 East Route A
Wentzville, MO 63385
www.gm.com

right or left front brakes to help keep the vehicle on track. These brake and engine interventions help realign the vehicle's actual path with that being steered by the driver.

Other standard crash-avoidance features include four-wheel antilock brakes for directional stability in emergency braking situations, and daytime running lamps for improved visibility. Safety belts, driver and

front passenger air bags, front and rear crush zones, and side-door beams are standard features designed to help protect occupants in the event of a crash.

In addition to being ISO-9001 certified, Wentzville Assembly has been recently ISO-14001 certified. ISO-14001 certification requires that an environmental management system be in place.

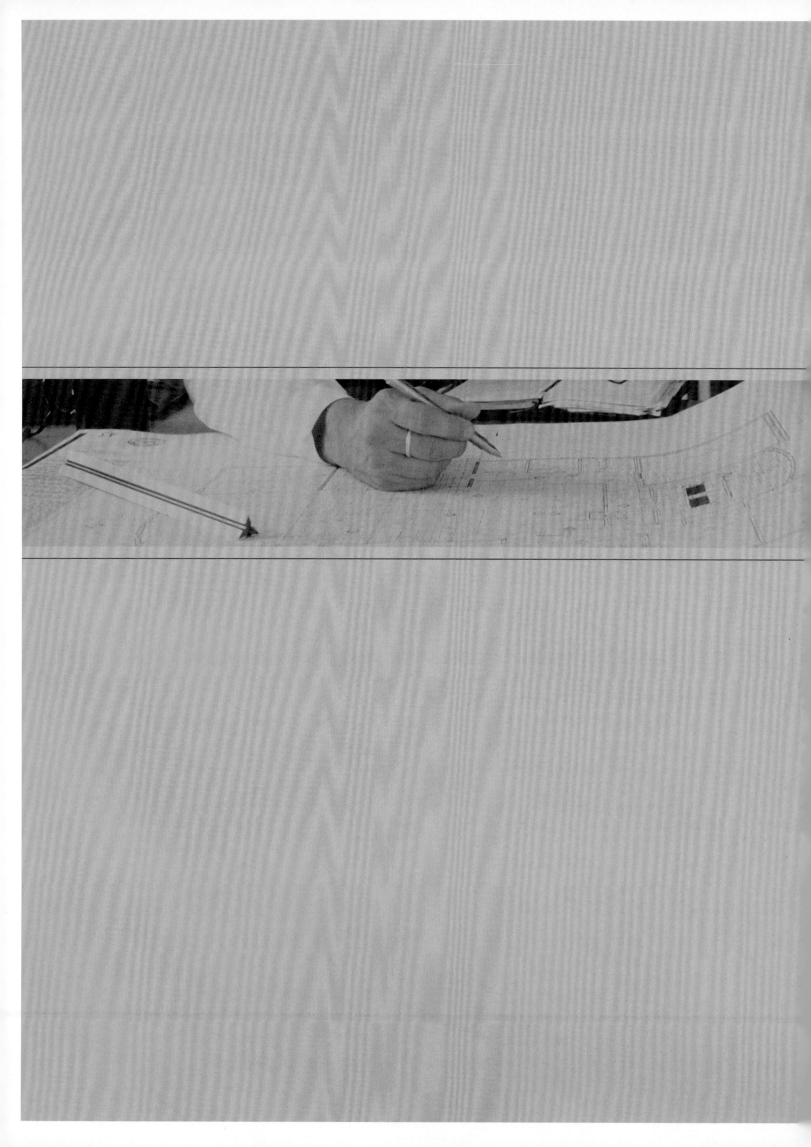

ARCHITECTURE
AND ENGINEERING

HELLMUTH, OBATA + KASSABAUM, INC.

This well-respected global architectural firm has received awards and recognition from the American Institute of Architects and Global Green USA for its environmentally sensitive architectural solutions as well as its commitment to design excellence.

The Alfred J. Arraj United States Courthouse in Denver, Colorado, was designed by Hellmuth, Obata + Kassabaum (HOK) using U.S. Green Building Council/Leadership in Energy and Environmental Design™ (USGBC/LEED™) guidelines.

Hellmuth, Obata + Kassabaum, Inc., (HOK) is among the world's largest, most diverse, and well-respected global architectural firms. Founded in 1955 in St. Louis, HOK is committed to design excellence, client service, and a collaborative approach to developing solutions for buildings and communities. The firm's expertise includes architecture, engineering, interior design, planning, lighting, graphics, facilities planning and assessment, and construction services.

Through its network of 21 offices worldwide, HOK serves diverse clients within the corporate, commercial, public, and institutional markets. As expansive as the HOK network has become, its philosophy remains focused on creating environments that enhance the quality of life for those who work, live, visit, and have fun in them.

For nearly 50 years, HOK has actively participated in the design of Missouri's future. From its offices in St. Louis and Kansas City, the firm has contributed to dozens of high-profile projects throughout the state. They include schools, churches, hospitals, courthouses, airports, stadiums, museums, laboratories, and corporate facilities. HOK employees support and contribute to their local communities and civic organizations as well.

With its unique and significant solutions, particularly to environmental design, HOK has made a profound and unmistakable impact on the architecture profession.

From the firm's pioneering initiatives in sustainable design to its groundbreaking efforts to diversify its practice areas, HOK has led important trends in architectural design and practice.

During the six years from 1998 through 2004, HOK designs were selected by the American Institute of Architects for its "Top 10 Green Projects" list of the most innovative "green" design solutions, including HOK's design for the Nidus Center for Scientific Enterprise in St. Louis. In addition, HOK is the first and only architectural firm to win the prestigious Designing a Sustainable and Secure World Award from Global Green USA, the U.S. affiliate of Mikhail Gorbachev's worldwide environment organization, Green Cross International, for its environmental efforts on behalf of the planet. The firm shares its resources and expertise with the design profession through *The HOK Guidebook to Sustainable Design*, published by John Wiley & Sons, Inc.

ATTRACTIONS

WORLDS OF FUN

With five continental-themed areas and the adjacent Oceans of Fun (the Midwest's largest tropically themed water park), Worlds of Fun features thrilling rides, entertaining shows, and great attractions for the whole family.

For more than three decades, Worlds of Fun and Oceans of Fun have generated excitement for the young and young at heart. These unique theme parks are two of the most popular tourist attractions in the Kansas City, Missouri, area.

Worlds of Fun offers a wide variety of rides, shows, and attractions. Its Americana, Europa, Africa, Scandinavia, and the Orient themed areas cover more than 175 acres. The park offers guests more than 50 rides and attractions, including ThunderHawk®, a six-story spinning thrill ride; Boomerang, a 12-story steel roller coaster; the 200-foot Detonator; and Timber Wolf®, a world-class wooden roller coaster. Camp Snoopy, one of only five in the country, also makes its home at Worlds of Fun. This kid-friendly area offers more than one acre of PEANUTS™-themed rides and attractions. Camp Snoopy is also

the only place in the Midwest to meet Snoopy and his gang each and every day, all season long.

In 1998, Worlds of Fun debuted its state-of-the-art steel roller coaster, the MAMBA®, one of the tallest, longest, and fastest in the world. The MAMBA's first hill takes riders more than 200 feet above the ground and shoots them toward the earth at up to 75 miles per hour. In 2004, the Spinning Dragons roller coaster opened to take thrill rides to the next level. As revolutionary as the MAMBA, this unique attraction features passenger cars that spin independently as they traverse the coaster's many hills and turns.

Adjacent to Worlds of Fun is Oceans of Fun, featuring more than 60 acres of water-related attractions. These include a million-gallon wave pool, eight water slides, a lazy floating river, special areas for children, an

adults-only pool with a swim-up cabana, waterslides, and more. There is also Hurricane Falls, a high-action superslide, and the newest attraction, Paradise Falls, featuring a 1,000-gallon bucket that fills and empties every five minutes on people below.

Worlds of Fun is owned and operated by Cedar Fair, L.P., which also owns and operates Cedar Point in Sandusky, Ohio; Michigan's Adventure near Muskegon, Michigan; Valleyfair! in Shakopee, Minnesota; Dorney Park & Wildwater Kingdom in Allentown, Pennsylvania; Knott's Berry Farm in Buena Park, California; and Geauga Lake near Cleveland, Ohio. Cedar Fair also manages Knott's Camp Snoopy at the Mall of America in Bloomington, Minnesota.

Right: Paradise Falls is only one of the water attractions at Oceans of Fun. Far right: The MAMBA® at Worlds of Fun is one of the tallest, longest, and fastest roller coasters in the world. "With more than 175 acres of rides, shows, and attractions, Worlds of Fun and Oceans of Fun continue to provide the Midwest with quality entertainment year after year," says Phil Bender, vice president and general manager.

SPECTATOR SPORTS
AND SPORTS ASSOCIATIONS

ST. LOUIS RAMS

In addition to being a world-champion football team, this local favorite involves itself extensively in programs for improving the lives of local youths, dedicating itself to sports clinics for kids, helping to develop youth leadership, and working extensively with underprivileged children.

The Rams established themselves in the National Football League (NFL) in 1937. Since owner and chairman Georgia Frontiere returned professional football to Missouri in 1995, the St. Louis Rams have sold out nine consecutive years of regular season and play-off home games. Two Super Bowl appearances in three years and a world championship have catapulted the team to elite status in the NFL. In January 2000, the Rams topped off the season-long NFL Century celebration with a brawling, heart-gripping victory over the Tennessee Titans in Super Bowl XXXIV. Led by quarterback Kurt Warner and running back Marshall Faulk, the team's explosive offense showed itself as one of the most prolific in the history of the NFL.

MAKING A POSITIVE IMPACT

The Rams have been the beneficiaries of great support from the St. Louis community. Eager to return the favor, the team established an active community outreach program, and Frontiere and minority owner Stan Kroenke also created the St. Louis Rams Foundation, a separate, nonprofit arm of the outreach program.

The Community Outreach Team supports positive change in the St. Louis region. Through the Community First program, area youth organizations are able to earn Rams T-shirts, a tour of the Edward Jones Dome, and seats to Rams games by implementing service projects. And through the team's focus on youth football, the Rams sponsor coaching clinics for junior high school and high school athletes, host the high school football division winners at a Rams home game, and provide resources for youth football programs.

The Rams have contributed more than $5 million in cash, grants, merchandise, and tickets to area charities. In addition, the team has helped raise thousands of dollars to improve the lives of area youth, and individual Rams players take active roles in efforts to better the community. The Rams are proud to be an integral part of St. Louis, both on and off the field.

Right: Wide receiver Torry Holt is deeply involved with the Bear Essentials program, which supports families with a parent who has cancer. He also helps with the Rams Reader Team, Get Into the Game, and the Diversity Awareness Partnership. Far right, top: Georgia Frontiere, chairman and owner of the Rams, pictured here with a few of her friends, runs or participates in many philanthropic organizations, including St. Louis Variety, which serves children with physical and mental disabilities. Far right, bottom: Among his many other civic engagements, running back Marshall Faulk donates time, funds, and energy to his Rams 28 Club, which rewards its members for making positive choices in life, with emphasis placed on attitude, education, and community service.

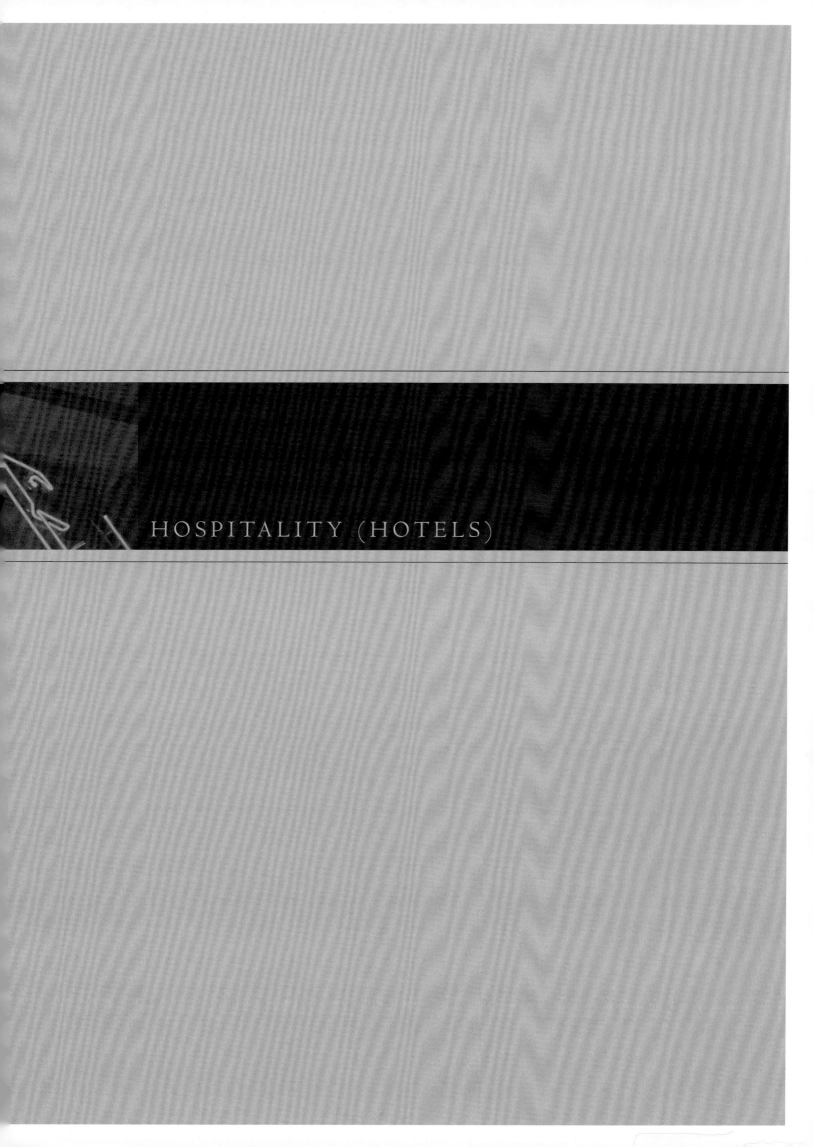

HOSPITALITY (HOTELS)

KANSAS CITY AIRPORT MARRIOTT

This highly regarded hotel is a professional's ideal, offering spacious rooms, fully wired for business; 15,000 square feet of flexible meeting space; hallmark Marriott service; and a convenient location on the grounds of Kansas City International Airport.

Marriott
KANSAS CITY AIRPORT

Conveniently located directly on the grounds of Kansas City International Airport, Kansas City Airport Marriott offers travelers first-class accommodations, amenities, and service. The hotel's relaxing atmosphere is enhanced by a beautiful man-made lake.

The Kansas City Airport Marriott opened in September 1974 as the 27th property in the young hotel business that became Marriott International, Inc. While Marriott International has grown to encompass an impressive portfolio of more than 2,600 properties worldwide, the Kansas City Airport Marriott remains one of the corporation's models of service to the business traveler.

When the hotel was built, it was a one-tower, 255-room facility designed to serve passengers from the recently opened Kansas City International Airport. The hotel quickly established a reputation for excellent service to business travelers, and expanded the facility in February 1989. The Kansas City Airport Marriott now boasts two towers, 378 guest rooms, and four suites to serve the 12 million passengers who use Kansas City International Airport annually, and remains the only hotel located on airport grounds.

Nearly 25 percent of the rooms have been designed as "The Room That Works," space created specifically for the modern business traveler. All such rooms are equipped with dual phone lines and multiple data ports with high-speed Internet connections. For the convenience of business travelers and local businesses alike, the hotel contains nearly 15,000 square feet of meeting space divided among 21 meeting rooms, including two 4,000-square-foot facilities that can accommodate up to 650 people at once. To ease the increasing demands made on business travelers, the hotel is undergoing a comprehensive renovation, complete with cutting-edge, high-tech upgrades. The meeting rooms were finished in early 2004, and the guest rooms will be started in early 2005.

The Kansas City Airport Marriott has been consistently recognized for its facilities and service. The hotel has earned three stars from *Mobil Travel Guide* as well as a three-diamond rating from AAA, and was recently ranked within the top 1 percent—25th worldwide—among Marriott International's properties in the Meeting Planner Satisfaction category.

The Kansas City Airport Marriott remains committed to serving the business traveler as the Kansas City region grows. Joe Novak, the hotel's director of marketing, vows that the hotel and its associates "will continue with the Marriott strategy of 'The Spirit to Serve' to ensure our clients are serviced today and into the future."

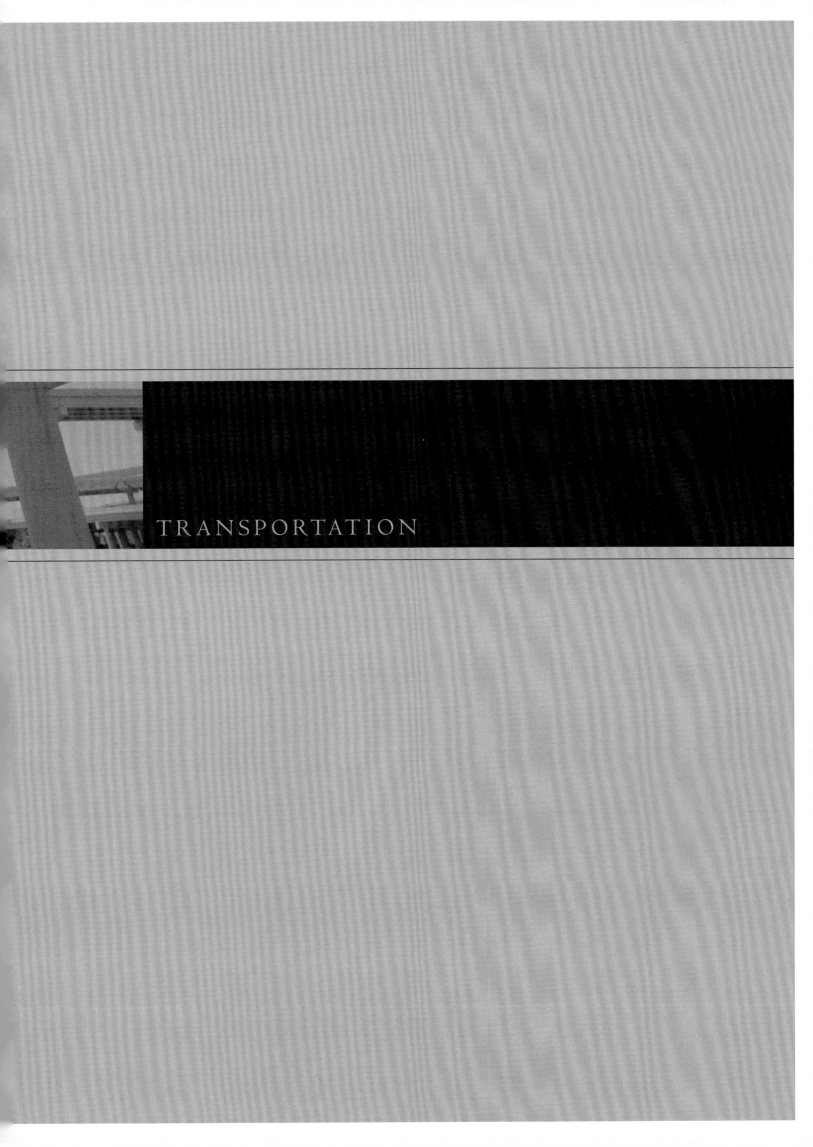

TRANSPORTATION

LAMBERT–ST. LOUIS INTERNATIONAL AIRPORT

What began as a launching spot for hot-air balloons has become one of the busiest commercial airports in the country, serving 10 major airlines, nine national or regional airlines, two major charter airlines, and six cargo carriers, with nearly half a million takeoffs and landings each year.

It is well established that from a tiny acorn a mighty oak may grow. A lesser-known phenomenon is that from a small hayfield a major airport may evolve. There is the belief that "if you build it they will come"—and that also has been the case at Lambert–St. Louis International Airport.

Albert Bond Lambert, a former major in the U.S. Army, possessed that vision and acted on it by developing an airfield on 160 acres of farmland in St. Louis County in June 1920. Over the next eight decades, this region has benefited from Lambert's early recognition of the growing importance of the aviation industry.

In those early years, Lambert's airfield, Lambert Field, soon grew to 550 acres on a site where St. Louis was clearly making its mark as one of the nation's aviation centers. In a sense, *Air Force One* came into being when Theodore Roosevelt, while visiting St. Louis in October 1910, became the first (former) president to ride in an airplane. St. Louis hosted the 1923 International Air Races, attracting the world's finest pilots. A young Charles Lindbergh was flying mail routes out of Lambert Field prior to his historic transatlantic flight, a venture that proclaimed to the world that St. Louis was committed to aviation.

In 1928, the City of St. Louis became the beneficiary of Lambert's vision and generosity with its acquisition of Lambert Field. The sale price of $68,352 represented only the amount of Lambert's purchase of the land for the airfield, and not his investment in the development of the land and construction of the facilities. Lambert Field became one of the first municipally owned airports in the United States. St. Louis had recognized the importance of the aviation industry and the need to build for the future.

The city's pioneering efforts were enhanced by geography. The area's earliest settlers were drawn to a location immediately south of the confluence of North America's two major rivers—the Mississippi and the Missouri. Manifest Destiny placed St. Louis at the heart of a growing nation. St. Louis would emerge as a railroad center and later as the junction of four interstate highways. Yet the seeds for the success of St. Louis in the 21st century were sown in the 1920s by Major Lambert.

In its early days, Lambert Field attracted hundreds of spectators intrigued by aviation. The airfield, shown here in 1934, later became Lambert–St. Louis International Airport.

From those seeds St. Louis has reaped a plentiful harvest over the years. The growth of commercial aviation was interrupted during World War II, but the military production of aircraft was prevalent in St. Louis with the presence of the Curtiss-Wright Corporation, the Robertson Aircraft Corporation, and McDonnell Aircraft Corporation. McDonnell—a forerunner of the McDonnell Douglas Corporation, which later merged with the Boeing Company—established its world headquarters at the northwest corner of Lambert Field and responded to Cold War market demands with its Phantom jets. However, McDonnell was also making news heard throughout the world with its contributions to the Mercury and Apollo space programs.

Lambert Field has physically grown throughout the years and experienced several name changes before becoming Lambert–St. Louis International Airport. The growth of any metropolitan area depends upon the strength of an airport's operations. Lambert has fulfilled that task by annually contributing $5.1 billion to the economy of the St. Louis region. Lambert has consistently ranked among the world's top airports in terms of passenger and operations totals.

Lambert is now in the midst of a $1.1 billion expansion project featuring the construction of a 2,000-foot runway to meet the demands of future growth and reduce costly weather-related delays. Of course, Lambert is facing the challenges

existing throughout the world in the wake of September 11th. Safety and efficiency have always been and will continue to be top priorities. This region will continue Major Albert Bond Lambert's tradition by building for the future at Lambert–St. Louis International Airport.

Top: Lambert–St. Louis International Airport's east terminal, completed in 1998, provides 220,000 square feet of space for use by Southwest Airlines and various charter carriers. Above: The new FAA control tower rises above Lambert's main terminal, which serves American Airlines and nearly a dozen other carriers.

KANSAS CITY AVIATION DEPARTMENT

This municipal department—which pays for itself—conducts all of Kansas City International Airport's matters of interest, from safeguarding more than 10 million passengers and 150,000 tons of freight and mail per year to entirely revamping the airport's terminal buildings.

With its drive-to-gate terminal design, Kansas City International Airport has been dubbed the world's most people-friendly airport. The airport, which is owned and operated by the Kansas City Aviation Department, spans more than 10,000 acres, and its three runways can accommodate up to 139 aircraft operations per hour.

The Kansas City Aviation Department, which owns and operates Kansas City International Airport (KCI), is charged with providing outstanding airport services in a safe and cost-effective manner. The department is an enterprise fund department of the City of Kansas City; is wholly supported by airport user fees; and is responsible for every aspect of running the 10,000-acre, triple-runway KCI complex.

The department's obligations are many. They include finding ways to increase demand for cargo and passenger service; ensuring that tenant contracts meet federal, state, and local regulations; safeguarding employees, clients, and passengers; and providing an airport police department. Among its many other duties are planning, designing, and building the airport's venues and facilities; collecting parking fees; maintaining and cleaning the buildings and grounds; and providing and servicing the fleet of vehicles needed for airport operations.

Driven by rising passenger and airline use and the need for updating the 30-year-old KCI facilities, the department proposed a $258 million improvement project to completely renovate the terminals, creating a more comfortable and user-friendly environment while enhancing passenger security and safety. The project, scheduled for completion in 2005, will relocate several airlines to other terminals to streamline traffic and relieve occasional congestion. It will also feature a synchronous optical network (SONET) ring to support electronic communications and optimize traffic patterns, more concession and retail space, wireless Internet service, larger departure lounges, upgraded security checkpoints, a new economy parking lot, a consolidated facility for rental cars, and art throughout the airport.

The Kansas City Aviation Department also owns and operates the city's downtown airport. When Charles Lindbergh dedicated Peninsula Field in 1927 as Kansas City Municipal Airport—now the Charles B. Wheeler Downtown Airport (MKC), serving corporate, charter, and recreational fliers—a facility the size of Kansas City International was barely imaginable. Three quarters of a century later, KCI serves as the focal point for air transportation and as a primary catalyst for economic growth in the greater Kansas City region.

UNIGROUP, INC.

One of the nation's largest transportation companies, UniGroup, Inc., coordinates all the logistics involved in household, corporate, and special-services relocations.

With a core business handling 600,000 shipments of household and other goods every year through its United Van Lines and Mayflower Transit subsidiaries, UniGroup, Inc., ranks as one of the nation's largest transportation companies. From its 38-acre headquarters in the St. Louis suburb of Fenton, UniGroup coordinates the transportation activities of an international network of independent agent-affiliates. In turn, these affiliates look to UniGroup's other operating companies for their needed goods and services, including information technology; corporate finance, travel, and communications; legal services; human resources; facilities management; and advertising and public relations.

UniGroup's roots extend back to the 1920s and the creation of a predecessor of United Van Lines called Return Loads Service, formed as the household goods moving business began to shift from railroads to over-the-road transportation. In 1947, the company was reorganized into United Van Lines,

and in 1987, it was again reorganized to create UniGroup. In 1995, UniGroup acquired Mayflower Transit, a household goods van line founded in 1927. According to the Gallup Moving Company Index, Mayflower has the highest unaided brand-name recognition in the industry.

TITANS OF THE INDUSTRY

United Van Lines and Mayflower Transit, while sister companies, are active competitors in the marketplace, with separate sales and operational activities. Between them, the two carriers handle approximately one in every three professional interstate relocations in the United States. Actual moving services are provided by the employees of the 900 United and Mayflower agencies located in cities throughout the country. An additional 500 representatives are located in Canada and other countries worldwide.

As United's and Mayflower's parent holding company, UniGroup earns yearly revenues of nearly $2 billion, making it one of the largest privately owned trucking groups in the United States. UniGroup is ranked by *Forbes* magazine as the 105th largest privately owned company in the nation. It is also the eighth largest private company based in the greater St. Louis area. In addition to United and Mayflower, UniGroup consists of Vanliner Group, one of the industry's largest specialty insurers, and Total Transportation Services, which sells and leases trucks and trailers and provides a full line of moving supplies and apparel.

Looking ever forward, UniGroup continues to expand its operating horizons, as exemplified by the creation in 1996 of UniGroup Worldwide, a global mobility management company that coordinates the services of international transportation on behalf of United Van Lines and Mayflower Transit.

Since 1927, Mayflower Transit has been moving families across town and around the world. Extensive experience and reliable, dedicated professionals have made Mayflower a leader in the moving business and in the relocation industry.

United Van Lines provides premium service without the premium price tag. For over 55 years, United has delivered quality service that is unsurpassed in the moving industry—making it one of America's top van lines.

CHERBO PUBLISHING GROUP

Cherbo Publishing Group's business-focused, art book–quality publications celebrate the vital spirit of America's past, present, and future.

Cherbo Publishing Group, Inc. (CPG), is North America's leading publisher of books for commercial, historical, civic, and trade associations. CPG products offer informative content, imaginative design, and quality materials and manufacture. From concept to completion, all publications are produced in CPG's facility using state-of-the-art equipment.

"Cherbo Publishing Group is a growing, privately held corporation with a talented staff and modern facilities," says company president, Jack Cherbo. "These assets, along with a professional sales and marketing team and a sophisticated network of suppliers and contractors, are part of CPG's recipe for success."

Jack Cherbo, a pioneer in the custom publishing industry, and Elaine Hoffman, CPG executive vice president, took Cherbo Publishing Group private in 1993. The company was formerly a division of Jostens Inc., a Fortune 500 company and the world's largest maker of school yearbooks and class rings. Today, CPG is based in Encino, California, and has regional offices in Philadelphia, Minneapolis, and Houston.

AMERICAN INDUSTRIES, AMERICAN INGENUITY

CPG publications—most of which are created in collaboration with a sponsoring agency—pay tribute to America's extraordinary business acumen and continuing legacy of innovation. These publications range from regional, architectural, preservation, and special interest books to state/regional business reports.

One of CPG's newest ventures is the Architectural series, beautifully illustrated books that celebrate the work of visionaries. Handsomely designed, these books demonstrate how city legislators, planners, designers, builders, and others have changed the urban landscape. Likewise, the Preservation & Smart Growth series illustrates the ways individual cities have managed to blend conservation efforts with structural growth.

CPG also publishes regional books that spotlight the country's most affluent and fastest growing metropolitan areas. Each book provides an in-depth look at a region's economic climate and industrial strengths.

CPG business reports highlight the economic advantages of individual cities or regions, while special interest publications celebrate anniversaries or special occasions for corporations, organizations, and professional and trade associations.

For more information about these and other new projects, or to find out how CPG can help you celebrate a special occasion or showcase your company or organization, contact Cherbo Publishing Group at (800) 854-9880 or visit www.cherbopub.com.

SELECT CPG PUBLICATIONS

STATE/REGIONAL SERIES

AMERICA & THE SPIRIT OF ENTERPRISE
Century of Progress, Future of Promise

ARKANSAS *The Natural State of Enterprise*

CALIFORNIA *Golden Past, Shining Future*

CONNECTICUT *Chartered for Progress*

DUPAGE COUNTY, ILLINOIS
Economic Powerhouse

INDIANA *Crossroads of Industry
and Innovation*

LUBBOCK, TEXAS *Gem of the South Plains*

MARYLAND *Anthem to Innovation*

MICHIGAN *America's Pacesetter*

NEW YORK STATE *Prime Mover*

NORTH CAROLINA *The State of Minds*

OKLAHOMA *The Center of It All*

PENNSYLVANIA *Keystone of the
New Millennium*

UPSTATE NEW YORK *Corridor to Progress*

WASHINGTON *New Discoveries,
New Frontiers*

**WESTCHESTER COUNTY,
NEW YORK**
Headquarters to the World

COMMEMORATIVE SERIES
CELEBRATE ST. PAUL *150 Years of History*

**BUILD IT AND THE CROWDS
WILL COME**
Seventy-Five Years of Public Assembly

THE EXHIBITION INDUSTRY
The Power of Commerce

**THE NATIONAL RURAL LETTER
CARRIERS' ASSOCIATION**
A Centennial Portrait

**THE NEW YORK STATE ASSOCIATION
OF FIRE CHIEFS**
Sizing Up a Century of Service

VISIONS TAKING SHAPE
*Celebrating 50 Years of the Precast/Prestressed
Concrete Industry*

**STATE/REGIONAL
BUSINESS REPORTS**
MINNESOTA REPORT 2004

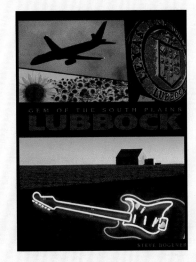

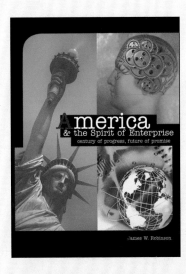

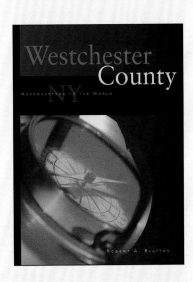

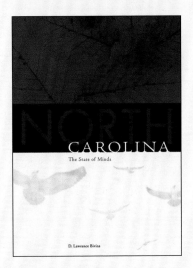

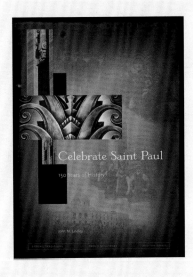

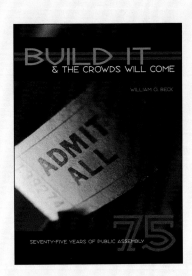

BIBLIOGRAPHY

Addison, J. Bruce (founder, Addison Biological Laboratory). Interview by author. July 16, 2003.

Allan, Robin. "Make Mine Marceline." *Animation World Magazine*, April 26, 2002.

Arnot, Charlie (vice president of communications and public affairs, Premium Standard Farms). Interview by author. June 17, 2003.

Artman, Pam (staff vice president of marketing services, Leggett & Platt, Inc.). Interview by author. September 24, 2003.

"Ask, Listen, Solve." *ABA Bank Marketing*, January 2003.

The Associated Press. "Tuition Is Free but Life Isn't Easy at 'Hard Work U'." *St. Louis Post-Dispatch*, March 23, 2003, sec. C.

"Association Renews Accreditation for Zoo." *St. Louis Post-Dispatch*, September 9, 2003, sec. B.

Barthels, Trudy (corporate communications manager, SSM Health Care) Interview by author. August 14, 2003.

Bavley, Alan. "Missouri to Adopt Disease Alert System." *The Kansas City Star*, April 1, 2003, sec. B.

Bavley, Alan, and Julie A. Karash. "Computer System Would Warn of Early Signs of Bioterrorist Attacks." *The Kansas City Star*, April 23, 2002, sec. A.

Beech-Nut. *The History of Beech-Nut Nutrition: Over a Century of Quality and Innovation.*

Bengel, Scott (plant manager, Stetson Hat Factory). Interview by author. September 3, 2003.

Berry, Tracey (communications office, Missouri Division of Tourism). Interview by author. December 9, 2003.

Buckley, Michelle. "Software Helps KCI Renovation Stay on Track for Completion." *The Business Journal of Kansas City*, August 2, 2002.

Burnes, Brian. "Century Later, Effects of 1903 Flood Still Resonate in KC." *The Kansas City Star*, May 31, 2003, sec. B.

Carey, Christopher. "Investors Bring Back Missouri Tree, Garden Center, Catalog Business." *KRTBN Knight Ridder Tribune Business News*, April 2, 2002.

Casey Newman, Sarah. "New Injection Neuters Animals without Surgery." *St. Louis Post-Dispatch*, June 14, 2003, sec. Lifestyle.

Cooper, Carrie. "Stunning New Technology: Premium Standard Farms Leads the Way with Carbon Dioxide Stunning." *Meat & Poultry*, March 2000.

Cordes, Henry J. "Change Wouldn't Keep Boats Afloat: Barges and State of Missouri Fight for Every Drop. St. Louis History of the Battle over the Missouri River." *Omaha World-Herald*, September 28, 2003, sec. A.

The Doe Run Company. *Primary Mining and Smelting Division: 2002 Annual Report to Our Community.* 2002.

_____. *Resource Recycling Division: 2002 Annual Report to Our Community.* 2002.

Drake, Susan M. *They Call Him John Q.: A Hotel Legend.* Memphis: Black Pants Publishing, 2002.

Elliott, Tina (senior manager, public communications, Anheuser-Busch). Interview by author. June 17, 2003.

Emerson. *The Lives We Touch: Emerson Charitable Trust Report.*

Ernst, Ashley. "Missouri Scientist Produces Herd-Specific Livestock Vaccines." *KRTBN Knight Ridder Tribune Business News*, April 24, 2001.

Ernsting, Kristi (general spokeswoman, Hallmark Cards, Inc.). Interview by author. September 17, 2003.

Farmer, Jack (senior vice president, Fleishman-Hillard). Interview by author. September 30, 2003.

Fondren, Gloria. "Moving Child Care into the 21st Century." News release, St. Louis Community College.

Foote, Andrea. "A Record of Success: August Busch III Named Recipient of Inaugural Beverage Lifetime Achievement Award." *Beverage World*, May 15, 2003.

Fowler, Jeff (director of media relations, St. Louis University). Interview by author. July 17, 2003.

Friedman, Steve. "Ebay Provides Columbia, Mo.-Area Automotive Insurer with Vehicle-Sales Avenue." *Columbia Daily Tribune*, March 12, 2002.

Gietschier, Steve. "A Visionary with a Mission: Johnson Spink Kept TSN on Course by Broadcasting Its Editorial Focus While Never Losing Sight of Its Past." *The Sporting News*, April 6, 1992.

_____. "Turning the Page on Another Chapter; As TSN Looks Ahead to Exciting Changes, It Takes a Look Back." *The Sporting News*, December 1, 1997.

Gilbert, Virginia Baldwin. "Botanical Society Will Move Here from Ohio; Deal Comes as Plum for St. Louis, Plant Biologists." *St. Louis Post-Dispatch*, June 4, 2002, sec. C.

Gillam, Carey. "Premium Standard Unveils New Hog Waste Facilities." Reuters News, July 19, 2002.

Hampel, Paul. "River City St. Louis Grew Up Hugging the Banks of the Mississippi—but Then Looked Away." *St. Louis Post-Dispatch*, November 28, 1999, sec. C.

Hargraves, Richard (spokesman, The Laclede Group). Interview by author. December 8, 2003.

Harris, Ron, and Pam Barnes. "Danforth Foundation Gambles on Success of Life Sciences; Grants to Groups Serving Others with Interests Will End." *St. Louis Post-Dispatch*, January 21, 2003, sec. A.

Hernandez, Tomas, Jr. "Collaboration in Construction." *Building Design & Construction*, April 2003.

Hickey, Kathleen. "Two Tech Wins." *Traffic World*, July 14, 2003.

"Hugh Steavenson; Founded Forrest Keeling Nursery." *St. Louis Post-Dispatch*, September 6, 2002, sec. B.

Hutchison, Liese L. "Made in St. Louis: From Airplanes to Silicon Wafers, Numerous Products Are Manufactured in St. Louis That Are Used throughout the World." *St. Louis Commerce Magazine*, October 2000.

Isaacson, Kathleen (communications manager, American Business Women's Association). Interview by author. September 23, 2003.

"Jack Henry Enters Partnerships." *Credit Union Journal* (June 23, 2003): 16.

Johnson, Robert (sales manager, Missouri Mulch). Interview by author. June 13, 2003.

Kerr, Candy (executive assistant, OCCU-TEC). Interview by author. November 5, 2003.

Kipp, Kevin. "Moving Ahead." *St. Louis Commerce Magazine*, October 2002.

Klise, Kate. "College Life Is a Job on Ozark Campus." *St. Louis Post-Dispatch*, October 4, 1992, sec. L.

Knox, Lisa. "New Option for Neutering Puppies is Fast, Less Invasive." *Lancaster New Era/Intelligencer Journal/Sunday News*, June 27, 2003.

Laclede Gas Company. *Annual Report to the Stockholders of the Laclede Gas Co. for the Fiscal Year Ended September 20, 1982.* 1982.

Lampitt, Elizabeth A. (administrative assistant, Laclede Gas Company). Interview by author. November 14, 2003.

Landis, David. "Street Smart: By Keeping It Simple, Edward Jones Enhances Its Image While Rivals Are Bloodied By Scandal." *Kiplinger's Personal Finance*, May 2003.

Lee, Thomas. "Movie Theaters Start Popping Back up as Ticket Sales Encourage Expansion Plans." *St. Louis Post-Dispatch*, April 26, 2003, sec. A.

Lewis, Lisa (spokeswoman, Beech-Nut). Interview by author. June 13, 2003.

Loschke, Jenell (public relations representative, sturgisword). Interview by author. July 17, 2003.

Manka, Lora (manager for public relations and publications, Lathrop & Gage). Interview by author. September 26, 2003.

Matreci, Patricia (media relations coordinator, St. Louis Community College). Interview by author. May 6, 2003.

Medina, Kerry. "All-American Celebration: Branson Welcomes the Herschend Family's Second Area Theme Park." *Travel Agent*, April 28, 2003.

Melcer, Rachel. "New CEO Puts Monsanto on a New Course; Grant Reorganizes Team, Puts Focus on Sales of Seeds and Genetic Traits." *St. Louis Post-Dispatch*, June 19, 2003, sec. C.

Merz, Bob (zoological manager for invertebrates, St. Louis Zoo). Interview by author. November 18, 2003.

"Metropolitan Area Digest." *St. Louis Post-Dispatch*, September 9, 2003, sec. B.

Mincer, Jilian. "Role Model Rose from Mix of Work, Family." *The Kansas City Star*, October 9, 2001, sec. D.

Moseley, Joe (vice president of public affairs, Shelter Insurance). Interview by author. July 14, 2003.

Muehlenkamp, Joe (director of media relations, Saint Louis University Health Sciences Center). Interview by author. December 4, 2003.

Murphy, Kevin. "College Puts Students to Work for Free Education." *The Kansas City Star*, March 17, 2003, sec. A.

Nichols, Nick (operations manager, the City of St. Louis Port Authority). Interview by author. November 13, 2003.

Nicklaus, David. "Local Port Officials Are Working to Increase St. Louis' Standing in the Industry." *St. Louis Post-Dispatch*, October 30, 2000, sec. C.

Oates, Bob. "The Baseball Bible: For 48 Years, It Was the Product of Colorful, Devoted Editor." *Los Angeles Times*, April 7, 1986, sec. 3.

Offerman, Robert (managing partner, Hochschild, Bloom & Company). Interview by author. September 22, 2003.

"Online Safety Training Now Available through OCCU-TEC Partners with EMUWorldWide of Eastern Michigan University." PR Newswire, January 8, 2002.

Poe, William. "Water Wars." *St. Louis Commerce Magazine*, October 2001.

Pollan, Michael. "Interview: Author Michael Pollan Talks about the History of the Apple." By Ketzel Levine. *NPR: Morning Edition*, June 5, 2001.

Posnanski, Joe. "Times Have Changed for *The Sporting News*." *The Kansas City Star*, June 22, 2003, sec. C.

Powell, Janet (spokeswoman, St. Louis Zoo). Interview by author. November 18, 2003.

Rice, Patricia. "Celebration to Honor the Legacy of Nursing Nuns." *St. Louis Post-Dispatch*, June 7, 1997, sec. Religion.

Rogers, John. "Price of College Admission: Backbreaking Labor." *Rocky Mountain News*, February 22, 1998, sec. 13A.

Rouch, Tracy (public relations manager, *St. Louis Post-Dispatch*). Interview by author. September 23, 2003.

St. Louis Community College. *Forty Years: A Light to the Community, a Reflection of Its People.* 2002.

"St. Louis Regional Technology Top 50: Plant & Life Sciences Companies, Forrest Keeling Nursery, Inc." *St. Louis Commerce Magazine*, September 2002.

Schmelder, Bill (director of marketing, Transentric). Interview by author. August 29, 2003.

Seely, Mike. "Sporting Snooze: A Leaner, Splashier *Sporting News* Struggles to Find Its Editorial Compass." *Riverfront Times*, June 25, 2003.

Shattuck, Harry. "Silver Dollar City Strikes It Rich." *Houston Chronicle*, December 3, 2000, sec. 2.

Shepard, Barbara (vice president of human resources and community relations, The Doe Run Company). Interview by author. May 27, 2003.

Singer, Sandy (public information officer, Lambert–St. Louis International Airport). Interview by author. November 14, 2003.

Sisters of Mercy Health System. *From Vision to Reality: Fulfilling the Plan.* 2003.

Sonderegger, John. "Turning a Page at Age 105, New-Looking *Sporting News* Battling Stiff Competition." *St. Louis Post-Dispatch*, June 28, 1991, sec. D.

Sonderman, John (president and chief executive officer, EDM Incorporated). Interview by author. September 15, 2003.

Sports Illustrated Editors. *Sports Illustrated 1999 Sports Almanac.* Boston: Little, Brown and Company, 1998.

Stier, Richard F. "Food Safety Is Good Business: Programs Should Not Be in a Dusty Binder on the Shelf. They Must Be Part of the Company Culture." *Food Engineering*, October 1, 2002.

Stluka, Mary (executive assistant, Jack Henry & Associates). Interview by author. September 15, 2003.

Stovsky, Renee. "Nuns Put Together a History of Caring." *St. Louis Post-Dispatch*, August 22, 2002, sec. North Post.

Strupp, Joe. "'Sporting' Ventures." *Editor & Publisher Magazine*, February 21, 2000.

Suhr, Jim. "Archeologist Probes River for Clues to Past; Waters Give Up Secrets of Sunken Boats Only to Swallow Them Up Again." The Associated Press, April 14, 2002.

Tesreau, Kerri, and Veronica Gielazauskas. "Entrepreneurship: A Driving Force in the New Economy." Missouri Economic Research and Information Center, March 2002.

Tuckey, Steve. "New Insurer Marketing Options." *Insurance Accounting*, December 3, 2001.

Uhlenbrock, Tom. "Students Pay Their Dues at This College." *St. Louis Post-Dispatch*, May 11, 2003, sec. T.

Vansickle, Joe. "Environmental Certification." *National Hog Farmer*, March 15, 2003.

Waldvogel, Chris. "A Grand Plan: SLU Entertains Community Support through the Art of Good Neighboring." *Universitas: The Magazine of Saint Louis University*, Spring/Summer 2003.

Whiteley, Larry (manager of corporation communications, Bass Pro Shops). Interview by author. November 13, 2003.

Wittenauer, Cheryl. "Fruit Tree Developer Looks to the Future." The Associated Press, January 29, 2003.

Wylie, Ann, Dawn J. Grubb, and Robert L. Dyer. *Missouri on the Eve of the Twenty-First Century.* Encino: Cherbo Publishing Group, Inc., 1999.

The Web sites of the following companies and organizations also were consulted for this book:

The Academy of American Poets, Addison Biological Laboratory, The African American Registry, Albrecht-Kemper Museum of Art, AMC Entertainment, Ameren, American Business Women's Association, Anheuser-Busch, The Annie E. Casey Foundation, Aquila, Audit Bureau of Circulation, Bass Pro Shops, Beech-Nut, BJC HealthCare, Boeing Company, Branson, Branson/Lakes Area Chamber of Commerce & Convention & Visitors Bureau, Branson USA Online, Brewer Science, Central Institute for the Deaf, Cerner Corporation, Charter Communications, City of Chillicothe, College of the Ozarks, Commerce Bank, Country Club Plaza, The Doe Run Company, Draper Laboratory, Drury Hotels, EDM Incorporated, Edward Jones, Emerson, *Engineering News-Record*, Enterprise Rent-A-Car, Express Scripts, Faultless Starch/Bon Ami Company, Fleishman-Hillard, Forrest Keeling Nursery, Graybar, Hallmark Cards, H&R Block, Harris-Stowe State College, Hochschild, Bloom & Company, Hoover's Online, Independent Stave Company, Jack Henry & Associates, Kansas City Ballet, Kansas City Chiefs, Kansas City Royals, Katy Central, Kirksville College of Osteopathic Medicine, Laclede Gas Company, Laclede Group, Lambert–St. Louis International Airport, Lathrop & Gage, Leggett & Platt, Inc., Lincoln University of Missouri, Mallinckrodt, The May Department Stores Company, MFA, Midwest Research Institute, Missouri Association for Advancing Manufacturing, Missouri Conservationist Online, Missouri Department of Agriculture, Missouri Department of Conservation Online, Missouri Department of Economic Development, Missouri Department of Elementary and Secondary Education, Missouri Department of Higher Education, Missouri Division of Tourism, Missouri Economic Research and Information Center, Missouri Economy, Missouri History, Missouri Mulch, Missouri School of Journalism, Missouri State Government, Missouri State Parks and Historic Sites, Monsanto, National Park Service, The Nelson-Atkins Museum of Art, Nestle Purina PetCare Company, OCCU-TEC, Outdoor World Incentives, Peabody Energy, Perry County Mutual Insurance Company, Pony Express National Museum, Premium Standard Farms, Pulitzer Inc., St. John's Health System, St. John's Mercy, St. Louis Blues, St. Louis Cardinals, St. Louis Children's Hospital, St. Louis Community College, St. Louis Convention & Visitors Commission, St. Louis Regional Growth and Commerce, Saint Louis Symphony Orchestra, Saint Louis University, St. Louis Zoo, Shelter Insurance, Silver Dollar City, Sisters of Mercy Health System, Small Business Survival Committee, Southwest Missouri State University, Spartech Corporation, *The Sporting News*, SSM Health Care System, Stark Bro's Nurseries & Orchards Co., Stetson Hat, Stone Hill Winery, Stowers Institute for Medical Research, Transentric, Travel Association of America, UniGroup, United States Court of Appeals for the 8th Circuit, University of Missouri–Kansas City, University of Missouri System, University Press of Kansas, Walton Construction Company, Washington University, Washington University School of Medicine, World Bird Sanctuary, World Cooperage.

INDEX

Addison Biological Laboratory, 69–70

Addison, J. Bruce, 69

Adventures of Huckleberry Finn, 4

Adventures of Tom Sawyer, The, 4

Agriculture, 18–19, 33–35

Albrecht-Kemper Museum of Art, 21, 23

Allegra-D, 11

Allen, Paul, 78, 81

AMC Entertainment, 9, 56, 59, 60

Ameren Corporation, 11

AmerenCIPS, 11

AmerenUE, 11

American Business Women's Association, 10, 95–96, 99

American Business Women's Day, 10, 95

American Multi-Cinema, 59

Andy's Seasoning, Inc., 130

Anheuser, Eberhard, 35

Anheuser-Busch Companies, Inc., 5, 16, 35–36, 41, 96, 128–29

Aquila, 116

Arkell, Bartlett, 38

Aspirin, 10

AstroDome, 9

AstroTurf, 9

Atchison, Topeka & Santa Fe Railroad Co., 93

Atlanta, 114

Atlantic Ocean, 7

Avis, 114

Babcock, Barry, 77

Baldknobbers Hillbilly Jamboree Show, The, 102

Barnes-Jewish Hospital, 64, 65

Bass Pro Shops, 109

Bayer CropScience, 27, 174–75

Beaham, Thomas G., 89

Beech-Nut Nutrition Corporation, 36, 38

Beer, 35–36

Benton, Thomas Hart, 5, 23

Berry, Albert, 6

Berry, Chuck, 10

Beverly Hillbillies, The, 9

Bib-Label Lithiated Lemon-Lime Soda, 7

Big Cedar Lodge, 109

Big Muddy Folk Festival, 29

BioKyowa Inc., 173

BJC HealthCare, 20, 65

Bloch, Henry, 55

Bloch, Richard, 55

Bloom, Melvin, 99

Blue Cross and Blue Shield of Missouri, 150

Blue Springs School District, 139

Boeing Company, 16

Bon Ami, 89

Boonville, 29

Boston, 81

Boswell, T. W., 39

Botanical Society of America, 11, 19

Braille, 4

Branson, 9, 101–02, 103

Brewer Science, 91

Brookings, Robert, 64

Brown v. Board of Education, 46

Budweiser, 5, 35

Bufton, Hilary A., Jr., 95

Bufton, Ruth, 95

Burlington Northern Santa Fe Railroad, 93

Busch, Adolphus, 35

Busch, August, 35–36

Busch, August, III, 36

Business Week, 21

Cable in the Classroom, 81

Café St. Louis, 8

Canada, 77

Cape Girardeau, 90

Carthage, 16, 87

Cataracts, 11

"Cave State," The, 29

Celebration City, 103

Center for Advanced Medicine, 65–66

Center for Excellence in Life Sciences Research, 19

Central Institute for the Deaf, 20

Central Missouri State University, 18, 134–35

Central Park, 29

Centric Group, 115

Cerner Corporation, 74, 81

Charles de Gaulle Airport, 113

Charter Communications, Inc., 16, 26, 77–78, 81, 166–67

Chesterfield, 99

Chicago, 8, 81

Child Development Center, 50

Churchill, Winston, 8

City of Kansas City, Missouri, 124–25

Clark, William, 15

Clayton, 16, 90

Cleft Palate and Craniofacial Deformities Institute, 66

Clemens, Samuel Langhorne, 4

Coca-Cola Company, 6, 70

Cole County Historical Museum, 25

College of the Ozarks, 49–50

Columbia, 45, 55, 60

Columbia University, 78

Commerce Bank, 10, 54–55

Cori, Carl Ferdinand and Gerty Theresa, 8

Country Club Plaza, 7, 56

Couzins, Phoebe Wilson, 5

Crayola Crayons, 85

Crock-Pot, 9

Crown Center, 84–85

Cytotec, 11, 70

Daily Star, 78

Danforth, William H., 38

Danforth Foundation, 63

Daniel Boone Home, 26

David's Bridal, 109

Defiance, 26

Disney, Walt, 6

District of Columbia, 109

Doe Run Company, 39, 41

Draper, Charles Stark, 5

Drury, Lambert, 105

Drury Inns, 105–06

Du Bourg, Louis William, 43

Durwood, Edward, 56, 59

Durwood, Stanley, 56

Durwood Theatres, 56

Eames, Charles, 6

Eastern Michigan University, 99

EDM, 94

Education, 20–21, 43–51

Edward Jones, 53–54

Eisenhower, President and Mrs. Dwight D., 8

Eliot, Thomas Sterns (T. S.), 7

Elman, Carolyn Bufton, 95

Elsberry, 34

Emerson, 16, 85, 87, 91, 96

Emerson, John Wesley, 85

Emerson Center, 91

Engineered Support Systems, 16

Enterprise Fleet Services, 114

Enterprise Rent-A-Car, 114–15, 119

Ewing Marion Kauffman Foundation, 95

Express Scripts, 16, 66, 162–63

Fairview Heights, Illinois, 94

Famous-Barr, 106, 109

Famous Clothing Store, The, 106

Faultless/Bon Ami Company, 89–90

Faultless Starch, 89

Fergason, James, 9

Filene's, 109

Finn, Huckleberry, 7

First Banks America, 16

First Hand Foundation, 81

Fleishman, Al, 96

Fleishman-Hillard, 96, 99

Foley's, 109

Forest Park, 25, 29, 103

Forrest Keeling Nursery, 34, 41

Forsythe, James, 49

Fort Leonard Wood, 16

Fortune 500, 16

Fortune magazine, 16

Fox Theatre, 25

France, 7

Franklin Covey, 95

Gage, John B. (Jack), 94

Gateway Arch, 9, 25, 28

Gemini 4, 9

General Motors Corp., 176–77

George K. Baum & Company, 146

George Washington Carver National Monument, 7

Giralda Tower, 56

Glenn, John, 9

G. Mallinckrodt & Company, 66

Gordon, Tad, 35

Gorup, Paul, 74

Graham, John, 96

Great Cathedral, 56

Green, Lemuel, 116

Grigg, Charles Leiper, 7

Gudmundsson, Skuli, 96

Habitat for Humanity, 60

Hall, Jerry, 73

Hall, Joyce Clyde, 83–85

Hall, Rollie, 83–84

Hall, William, 84

Hallmark Cards, 8, 83–85, 91, 96

Hallmark Hall of Fame, 84

Hammons, James Quentin, 105

H&R Block, 55, 60

Hannibal, 7, 26

Harms, Dennis, 35

Harris Teachers College, 4

Harry S. Truman Library, 26

Hartsburg, 29

Health care, 20, 62–71

Hearst, William Randolph, 78

Heart transplant, 9

Held, Jim and Betty, 36

Hellmuth, Obata + Kassabaum, Inc., 180

INDEX

Henry, Jack, 73

Hermann, 36

Herschend, Hugo and Mary, 102–03

Herschend, Jack, 103

Herschend, Peter, 103

Herschend Family Entertainment Corporation, 103

Hertz, 114

Heydon, Duncan, 96

Higher Education Act, 50

Hillard, Bob, 96

Hiroshima, 7

Hochschild, Peter, 99

Hochschild, Bloom & Company, 99

Hoechst Marion Roussel, 11

Holden, Bob, 19

Holiday Inn, 105

Holl, Steven, 23

Home Pride, 11

Hostess, 11

Houston, 9

Humansville, 90

Illig, Cliff, 74

Illinois River, 111

Imperial Packing Company, 38

Independence, 26

Independent Stave Company, 39, 41

Internal Revenue Service, 55

International Game Fish Association, 109

Interstate Bakeries Corporation, 11

Iron Curtain speech, 8

I-70 Series, 10

Jack Henry & Associates, 73–74

J. A. Folger Company, 8

Jefferson, Thomas, 44

Jefferson City, 5, 25, 46

Jefferson County, 111

Jefferson National Expansion Memorial, 25

Jesse James Bank Museum, 26

John F. Kennedy Airport, 113

John Q. Hammons Hotels, 105

Jones, Edward D., Sr., 54

Jones, Edward D. "Ted," Jr., 54

Joplin, 91

Joplin, Scott, 5

Journalism school, 45

Kaiser, Ray, 6

Kansas City, 5, 7, 8, 9, 10, 11, 16, 19, 20, 34, 45, 54, 55, 56, 59,
    89, 90, 93, 96, 116

Kansas City Airport Marriott, 192

Kansas City Aviation Department, 198

Kansas City Ballet, 21, 23

Kansas City Chiefs, 28

Kansas City Health Department, 74

Kansas City International Airport, 59–60

Kansas City Monarchs, 7

Kansas City Royals, 10, 28

Katy Trail State Park, 28–29

Kaufmann's, 109

Keeling, Forrest, 34

Kent, Jerry, 77

Kirksville, 50

Kirksville College of Osteopathic Medicine, 50

Korean War, 8

KU Center for Management Education, 96

Kwik Krop Fruit Tree, 34

Laclede Gas Company, 116

Laclede Group, The, 116

Lake of the Ozarks, 29

Lake Taneycomo, 102

Lambert, Albert, 113

Lambert–St. Louis International Airport, 21, 113–14, 196–97

Lambert–St. Louis Municipal Airport, 113

Lathrop, Gardiner, 94

Lathrop & Gage, 93–94

Leadville, Colorado, 106

Lebanon, 39

Leggett, J. P., 87

Leggett & Platt, 16, 87, 89, 91

Lewis, Meriwether, 15

Lewis and Clark Rendezvous, 29

Lewis Howe Co., 7

Liberty, 26

Life Sciences Research Trust Fund, 19

Lincoln Institute, 46

Lincoln University, 46, 49

Lindbergh, Charles, 7

Lindenwood University, 140

Lipe, Raymond and Walter, 38

Little House on the Prairie, 5

Long, Francis Reid, 54

Los Angeles, 81

Louis and Clark expedition, 29

Louisiana Purchase, 15

Louisiana Purchase Exposition World's Fair, 6

Madison County, Illinois, 111

Mallinckrodt, 66, 69, 70

Mallinckrodt, Edward, 66

Mallinckrodt, Gustav, 66

Mallinckrodt, Otto, 66

M&M's, 8

Manhattan Project, 70

Manufacturing, 82–91

Maple Leaf Club, 5

Maple Leaf Rag, 5

Marceline, 26

Maris, Roger, 11

Mark Twain Boyhood Home and Museum, 26

Marshall Plan, 7

Marvel Cave, 102

Maryland Heights, 16, 66

Maverick Tube Corporation, 170–72

May, David, 106

May Department Stores Company, 16, 106, 109

Mayflower Transit, 115, 116

McDonnell Douglas Aircraft Corporation, 8, 9, 113

McGwire, Mark, 11

McNeal, Theodore, 9

McQuarter, Hobart, 101

Medicare-Glaser, 66

"Meet Me in St. Louis," 29

Mercury MR-3 spacecraft, 9

Meston, Alexander, 85

Meston, Charles, 85

Mexico, 77

Mexico, Missouri, 54

Michelob, 35

Michelob Ultra, 36

Microsoft, 78, 81

Midwest Research Institute, 8, 10, 20

Milnot Company, 38

Miss America, 11

Mississippi River, 5, 33, 93, 111

Missouri, 4–11, 14–29

    agriculture and, 33–35

    biotechnology and, 70

    business-to-business services and, 96–99

    communications and, 77–78

    construction and, 59–60

    education and, 42–51

    energy and, 116–19

    finance and, 53–55

    food processing and, 35–38

    forestry and, 39

    health care and, 63–70

    hospitality and, 105–06

    information technology and, 73–77

    insurance and, 55–56

    manufacturing and, 82–91

    media and, 78–81

    mining and, 39, 41

    professional services and, 93–96

    real estate and, 56–59

    retail and, 106–09

    tourism and, 101–05

    transportation and, 111–16

    utilities and, 116

Missouri Botanical Garden, 119

Missouri Credit Union Association, 20, 144–45

Missouri History Museum, 25

Missouri Hospital Association, 154–55

Missouri-Kansas-Texas Railroad, 28

Missouri Mulch, 41

Missouri River, 15, 111

Missouri School for the Blind, 4

Missouri Southern State University, 91

Missouri State Board of Education, 20

Missouri State Capitol, 25

Missouri State Capitol series, 5

Missouri Western State College, 138

Monett, 73

Money Magazine, 21

Monsanto, 6, 9, 10, 11, 19, 70

Monsanto Fund, 70

Montreal, 10

Morris, Johnny, 109

Mother Goose Rhymes, 89

MovieTickets.com, 59

Multicultural Communications Scholarships program, 99

Municipal Opera, 25

Museum of Westward Expansion, 25

Musial, Stan, 8

Nagasaki, 7

National Fish and Wildlife Foundation, 109

National Prescription Administrators, 66

National Urban League, 119

Naval Aviation Museum Foundation, 119

Negro World Series, 7

Nelson-Atkins Museum of Art, The, 23

Nesbitt, John, 89

Nestle Purina PetCare Company, 38

New York, 7, 81, 113

New York Journal, 78

New York Life, 66

New York Stock Exchange, 106

New York World, 78

Nichols, Jesse Clyde, 56

Nobel Prize, 7, 8

North Atlantic Treaty Organization (NATO), 8

INDEX

OCCU-TEC, 96, 99

Old Courthouse, 25

Olympic Games, 6. See also Summer Olympics.

Omnicom Group, 96

Outdoor World, 109

Owl and the Pussy Cat, The, 89

Ozark Mountains, 101, 109

Paris, 113

Parkmoor, 7

Parks Air College, 44

PathNet, 74

Patterson, Neal, 74

Peabody, Francis S., 119

Peabody Energy, 116, 119

PGI & Associates, 74

Platt, C. B., 87

Pleasant Hill, 116

Point Lookout, 49

Pony Express, 5

Pony Express Museum, The, 25

Port of Metropolitan St. Louis, 111, 113

Posilac, 11

Powell Symphony Hall, 25

Powers, Lawrence, 90

Premium Standard Farms, 34–35, 41

Prohibition, 35, 39

Pulitzer, Joseph, 78

Pulitzer Inc., 78

Pulitzer prizes, 6, 78

Pumpkin Festival, 29

Queeny, Edgar, 70

Queeny, John Francis, 70

Ralston Purina, 9, 38

Rapid Refund, 55

Reagan, Ronald, 10, 95

Redbook, 21

Rival Manufacturing Company, 9

Robinsons-May, 109

Rocheport, 29

Rock 'n' Roll Hall of Fame, 10

Rolla, 91

Roosevelt, Franklin D., 7

Ross, Donald, 115

Roundup, 70

St. Charles, 28

St. Charles Riverfront Station, 94

St. Ignatius Loyola, 44

St. John's Mercy Medical Center, 64

St. Joseph, 5, 9, 23, 25

St. Joseph Lead Company, 39, 41

St. Louis, 4, 5, 6, 7, 8, 9, 10, 11, 15, 16, 19, 20, 25, 26, 28, 29, 35, 36, 45, 53, 55, 63, 64, 66, 70, 77, 78, 85, 90, 94, 106, 111, 113, 115, 116

Saint Louis Art Museum, 25

St. Louis Blues, 26, 28

St. Louis Board of Education, 5

St. Louis Cardinals, 7, 8, 10, 11, 28

St. Louis Children's Hospital, 64, 66

St. Louis College, 13

St. Louis Community College System, 50

St. Louis Police Department, 6

St. Louis Post-Dispatch, 45, 78, 81

St. Louis Rams, 11, 26, 94, 188

Saint Louis Symphony Orchestra, 21, 23, 25, 119

Saint Louis University, 19, 44

Saint Louis University's Health Sciences Center, 9

Saint Louis University's School of Nursing, 11

St. Louis World's Fair, 6, 29, 103, 106

St. Louis Zoo, 103, 105

Saint Luke's Health System, 19, 156–57

St. Mary's Church, 63

St. Mary's Infirmary, 64

St. Regis Seminary, 4

Sammy Lane Resort, 101

Sanus, 66

Sawyer, Tom, 7

Scott, Dred, 4

Scott Joplin Ragtime Festival, 29

Scripps League Newspapers, 78

Sea World Orlando, 94

Sedalia, 28, 29

7UP, 7

Seville, Spain, 56

Sheldon Memorial Concert Hall, 25

Shelter Insurance, 55–56, 60

Shepard, Alan, 9

Silver Dollar City, 9, 103

Sisters of Mercy Health System, 64

Sisters of St. Mary, 63–64

62nd and 65th Colored Infantries, 46

Smithsonian Institution, 103

Society of Jesus, 44

Solar Energy Research Institute, 10

Sollomi, Phillip, 8

Southeast Missouri Hospital, 22, 158–59

South Korea, 8

Southwest Missouri State Bears, 26

Southwest Missouri State University, 23, 136–37

Spartech Corporation, 90

Spink, Alfred H., 78

Spink, C. C. Johnson, 81

Spink, Charles, 81

Spink, J. G. Taylor, 81

Spinks, Michael and Leon, 10

Spirit of St. Louis, 7

Sporting News, The, 26, 78, 81

Springfield, 16, 19, 26, 109

SSM Health Care System, 64, 70

Stanley Cup, 26, 28

Stark, James Hart, 33

Stark Bro's Nurseries & Orchards Company, 33–34

Stark Golden Delicious apple, 34

Stark Red Delicious apple, 34

Steavenson, Hugh A., 34

Stephen Bufton Memorial Educational Fund, 99

Stetson hats, 9

Still, Andrew Taylor, 50

Stokes, Patrick, 36

Stone Hill Winery, 36

Stowers Institute for Medical Research, 20

Strowger, Almon Brown, 5

Student Life, 45

Summer Olympics, 10, 29

Super Bowl, 11, 26

Table Rock Dam, 102

Taylor, Andrew "Andy," 114–15

Taylor, Jack, 114

Taylor family, 119

Teasdale, Sara, 6

Tender Vittles, 9

Tennessee Titans, 11

Thomas J. Lipton Company, 8

Times Mirror Company, 81

Tracker Boats, 109

Transentric, 77

Trans World Airlines, 113

Truman, Harry S., 7, 8

Tucson, 78

Tums, 7

Turner, Debbye, 11

Twain, Mark, 4, 7

Tyco International, 69

UniGroup, Inc., 115–16, 199

Union Pacific, 77

Union Station, 94

United States, 77

United Van Lines, 115, 116

United Way, 109

University of Kansas School of Business, 96

University of Missouri–Columbia, 6, 9, 69

University of Missouri–St. Louis, 9

University of Missouri System, 44–45

U.S. Department of Education, 20

U.S. Department of Energy, 10

U.S. News & World Report, 20

U.S. Secretary of Education, 20

U.S. Soil Conservation Service, 45

U.S. Supreme Court, 4, 46

UtiliCorp United, 116

Vulcan Ventures, 81

Wal-Mart, 96

Walt Disney's Home Town Museum, 26

Walton, Greg, 59

Walton Construction Company, 59–60

Washington, Missouri, 99

Washington University, 5, 10, 45–46, 64, 65

Washington University School of Medicine, 8, 11, 64, 65

Waste Land, The, 7

Westminster College, 8

WEW, 6

Whitaker & Co., 54

White, Ed, 9

Wilder, Laura Ingalls, 5

William Barr Dry Goods Company, 106

Williams, Walter, 6, 45

Wishbone, The, 8

Wonder bread, 11

Wonders of Wildlife National Museum, 109

Wood, Howard, 77

World Series, 7, 10, 28, 81

Worlds of Fun, 184

World War II, 70, 85, 94–95, 113

Zieley, David, 38

Zoological Society of St. Louis, 103

Zoo/Museum District Tax, 103

MISSOURI ORIGINALS

Pages 4–5

Top, left to right: Mark Twain, © Dictionary of American Portraits; Pony Express, © Kansas City Library; Almon Brown Strowger, © Science & Society Picture Library; Scott Joplin, © Hulton Archive/Getty Images.

Bottom, left to right: Dred Scott, © Dictionary of American Portraits; braille, © SuperStock; Eads Bridge, © G. E. Kidder Smith/CORBIS; Laura Ingalls Wilder, © Bettman/CORBIS.

Pages 6–7

Top, left to right: Walt Disney, © Hulton Archive/Getty Images; Sara Teasdale, © Underwood & Underwood/CORBIS; sliced bread, © Index Stock Imagery, Inc.; Harry S. Truman, © Dictionary of American Portraits.

Bottom, left to right: Charles Eames, © CORBIS; Wilber Joe Rogan of the Kansas City Monarchs, © National Baseball Hall of Fame; Charles Lindbergh and the *Spirit of St. Louis*, © CORBIS; George Washington Carver, © Dictionary of American Portraits.

Pages 8–9

Top, left to right: Stan Musial, © Bettman/CORBIS; Theodore McNeal, © Missouri State Archives; Gateway Arch, © Bettman/CORBIS; cowboy, © Royalty-Free/CORBIS.

Bottom, left to right: Drs. Carl Ferdinand and Getty Theresa Cori, © Bettman/CORBIS; astronauts Ed White and James McDivitt inside Gemini 4, © NASA; liquid crystal display, © Royalty-Free/CORBIS.

Pages 10–11

Top, left to right: aspirin, © Royalty-Free/CORBIS; solar panels, © Royalty-Free/CORBIS; dairy cows, © Royalty-Free/CORBIS; Torry Holt of the St. Louis Rams, © AFP/CORBIS; patient, © Royalty-Free/CORBIS.

Bottom, left to right: Michael Spinks, © Bettman/CORBIS; ATM card, © Royalty-Free/CORBIS; Debbye Turner, © www.debbyeturner.com; Mark McGwire, © Reuters New Media Inc./CORBIS; purple coneflowers, © Royalty-Free/CORBIS.

cherbo publishing group, inc.

TYPOGRAPHY

Principal faces used: Centaur MT, designed by Bruce Rogers in 1926; Adobe Garamond, designed by Robert Slimbach in 1989, which was derived from previous designs by Claude Garamond, Jean Jannon, and Robert Granjon; Futura, designed by Paul Renner in 1927; and Scala Sans, designed by Martin Majoor in 1993.

HARDWARE

Macintosh G4 desktops, digital color laser proofing with Xerox Docucolor 12, digital imaging with Creo EverSmart Supreme.

SOFTWARE

QuarkXPress, Adobe Illustrator, Adobe Photoshop, Adobe Acrobat, Microsoft Word, Eye-One Pro by Gretagmacbeth, Creo Oxygen, FlightCheck.

CTP, PRINTING, AND BINDING

Performed by Friesens of Altona, Manitoba, Canada, and Neche, North Dakota, USA.

PAPER

Text Paper: #80 Garda Gloss. Bound in Rainbow® recycled content papers from Ecological Fibers, Inc. Dust Jacket: #100 Sterling-Litho Gloss.